Nelly & the Mother Line

Nelly & the Mother Line

Roaming the Maritimes, Finding 9 Generations of Acadian Mothers

by Nancy Boudrot Spear

Mt. Nittany Press
Lemont   Berlin

Printed in the United States of America

Published by Mt. Nittany Press,
an imprint of Eifrig Publishing,
PO Box 66, Lemont, PA 16851.
Knobelsdorffstr. 44, 14059 Berlin, Germany

For information regarding permission, write to:
Rights and Permissions Department,
Eifrig Publishing,
PO Box 66, Lemont, PA 16851, USA.
permissions@eifrigpublishing.com, 888-340-6543.

Library of Congress Cataloging-in-Publication Data

Spear, Nancy Boudrot
  Nelly & the Mother Line, Roaming the Maritimes, Finding 9
  Generations of Acadian Mothers, by Nancy Boudrot Spear
  p.   cm.

Paperback: ISBN 978-1-63233-208-0
Hardcover: ISBN 978-1-63233-209-7
Ebook: ISBN 978-1-63233-210-3

    1. Memoir 2. Genealogy 3. History - Acadians 4. History - Canada
    5. Travel - Nova Scotia 6. Travel - Eastern Canada

I. Spear, Nancy Boudrot, II. Title.

23 22 21 20 2019

5 4 3 2 1
Printed on acid-free paper. ∞

For Bud,

Charlie, Kate, and Sally;
Eliza, Ava, Max,
Finn, Anya, and Asha

ACKNOWLEDGMENTS

Writing this book has been a journey that many shared with me. For their help and spirit of adventure, I give my deepest thanks.

Bud, my husband and traveling companion, cheered me on and gave loving support and understanding. Your enthusiasm for all things Acadian, and willingness to roam the Maritimes with me made the adventures twice as much fun. Thank you, always.

Special gratitude goes to *Janet Somerville*, editor and great friend, for all those Friday mornings at East Simpson discussing the book and new directions Your countless readings and advice were invaluable, and your friendship is a gift.

Harry Thurston was an inspiration in writing workshops, and in discussions outside of class. You also gave me the push I needed when you said, *Get it out there. It's ready.*

Stephen White shared his store of Acadian genealogy with patience, giving information and insight into Acadian families and their history. You constantly astonished me with the amount of information you carry, and the great dedication you have to preserving that knowledge so that many can learn from it.

Charlie Dan Roach provided the list of my nine grandmothers, and answered a wealth of Cheticamp questions during visits and via telephone. It's thanks to you that I have a broader understanding of the post Deportation era in Cape Breton.

To *Josette Boudreau Marchand*, and all the welcoming people of Isle Madame, *John Brown* and the folks of the Annapolis Valley, the historians at Fort Beausejour, *Jeanne-Doris LeBlanc*, who solved the mystery of my grandmother's name, the waitress who taught me how to make Acadian chowder, *Wilfred, Fredie* and *Rose Burns*, who welcomed us and shared knowledge of the Burns family, *John Aucoin*, who drove us to Nelly's childhood land, *Marc Lavoie* and the archeological work at the Belle Isle Marsh, *Robert Campbell*, whose blog entry opened up the world of Marie Madeleine Bois, and to the women at the Beaton Institute for help with the Robin ledgers, I give a special thanks.

To *Molly Hoben* and *Glenda Martin*, for reviewing the book and your encouragement, *Penny Eifrig*, for your care and guidance through the publishing process, and *Emily Snyder* for your graphic design expertise—thank you.

And to all the many unnamed Maritimers who helped and encouraged me along the way, you're the reason those who travel to eastern Canada return home saying, *The place is beautiful and the people are wonderful.*

Merci.

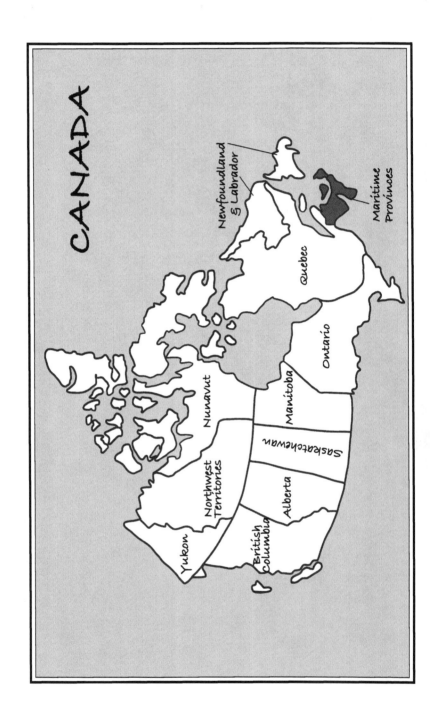

CANADA

Newfoundland & Labrador

Maritime Provinces

Quebec

Ontario

Nunavut

Manitoba

Saskatchewan

Northwest Territories

Alberta

Yukon

British Columbia

Maritime Provinces

Chéticamp
Sydney
Isle Madame
Cape Breton Island
PRINCE EDWARD ISLAND
Charlottetown
NOVA SCOTIA
Halifax
NEW BRUNSWICK
Digby
Saint John
Ferry

Part One

Part Two

On Nelly's Porch

Where are your people from? Your ancestors? I'm asked, and almost sing the answer. "Nova Scotia, New Brunswick, Prince Edward Island, Cape Breton Island — Canada's Maritimes." "And before that?" "France, and Scotland and Ireland, but the French were the first to arrive in North America. They were the Acadians." "And I don't mean Canadians," my granddaughter likes to add.

I'd never heard of the Acadian people, their voyages from France to Canada, and their lives in North America until I was in high school, and assigned to read the epic poem, *Evangeline*, by Henry Wadsworth Longfellow. The poem tells the story of the 1755 British expulsion of the Acadians from the Nova Scotia lands they'd loved and farmed for more than 100 years. Longfellow focused on the fictional Evangeline's long search to find her husband after they were separated on the Nova Scotia shore and displaced to the American colonies. He ends the poem, written in 1847, with Evangeline and her husband Gabriel's eventual sad reunion.

My lack of knowledge of the Acadians was despite our yearly trips to visit my mother's parents, Mary O'Brien and Duncan Lorimer, in Nova Scotia. They were Irish and Scottish, and *no-card-playing on Sundays* Presbyterians. Though they were fun-loving, and we were on vacation, the cribbage board always stayed in the kitchen table drawer on the Sabbath. My brother and I spent idyllic summers at our grandparents' cottage on the iron oxide-colored shores of the Northumberland Strait, looking across the water to Prince Edward Island. Though there were French areas nearby, we were never taken into any of them. Ethnic groups lived more separately then, and unless one of his brothers traveled to Nova Scotia with us, my father was the only Frenchman around.

My father's parents were French-speaking Acadians who left Cape Breton Island on the far reaches of Nova Scotia to emigrate to the United States. His mother, Nelly Burns, was from Friar's Head, near Margaree, on the Gulf of Saint Lawrence, and his father, Frederick Boudrot, was raised in West Arichat, on Isle Madame—an archipelago on the Atlantic Ocean side of the Island.

Nelly was a widow when I knew her. Frederick died in his sixties, leaving her as the matriarch in the large brown house on Faxon Street in Newton, Massachusetts. This was the house where my father grew up. My family lived about ten minutes away, but Faxon Street was where the action was. It functioned like a rambling boarding house, only all the residents were relatives, and I have no idea who took part in anything financial—or made any of the major maintenance decisions. Nelly had five children. Her daughter was married and living in Ohio, and my father, her fourth child, had a

15

stable marriage, and was in his own home with children and a loving wife.

Everyone else was either living in the Faxon Street house, or was there on an extended stay. One uncle, with his wife and young child, were there full time. A divorced uncle's children, my adored cousins, were brought up in the Faxon Street house, and a third uncle, also divorced, was frequently there. Despite the assortment of people populating the place, to me, it was always Grandma's House.

Nelly was barely five feet tall and wrapped her daily apron around a sturdy body. Her coarse white hair was carefully woven into a long braid and wound around the back of her head, but there were always sprigs of hair that escaped their intended place and softened her broad face. Her laughter didn't come often, but there were daily smiles, and she could be conspiratorial. "Don't tell your mother I let you stay up till after midnight to see the New Year in," she whispered in my ear when I was a young child staying with her and had never been up that late before.

When I spent the night there, I shared her bed, and quietly curled up in the dim light, watching as she stood across the room beside the stout chestnut dresser, methodically removing the wavy hairpins from her hair, then laying them beside the photo of her portly, red-headed, dead husband—my unknown grandfather. Her rope of braid dropped half-way to her waist, and she'd pull it apart to let the long mane free. There, in the fading light stood an ancient Rapunzel in a flannel nightgown, until she gathered in the flowing folds and became my grandmother again.

Lying in what seemed like a very big bed with too many blankets, I hardly moved, frightened by the crucifix hung above me on the bedroom wall. My little Protestant self looked at it only once to take in its gruesomeness. By standing on the pillows to examine it before Nelly came into the room, I satisfied my curiosity and sealed my resolve to never look at it again. But I always watched as Nelly got down on her knees and did a round on her rosary beads. Her fingers moved from bead to bead as her lips formed silent words, then the bed would groan as she leaned heavily into the mattress to get back to her feet and into our communal space. Nelly was deeply religious, and I now wonder how she dealt with those divorced uncles and my father, her favorite child everyone says, with his Protestant wife and children.

Once, when I was quite small, she took me to her church, *Saint Jean l'Evangelist*, to have my throat blessed. Just in case, I guess. I think I was supposed to keep quiet about this, but I described the whole mysterious event to my mother when I arrived home. Although I didn't have the words to describe it fully, I had the awe, and my own interpretation. My mother listened, but let it go. Or maybe not, since I was never taken to church by Nelly again. As an adult, out of respect, or maybe guilt for having squealed on her about the throat blessing, I've lit a candle for her in every Catholic church and cathedral I've ever visited across Europe and North America.

And whenever I think of Nelly, the Faxon Street porch with its rocking chairs that ran the full length across the front of the big brown house comes to view. It was a gathering place. Mid-afternoons, when their daily chores were finished and before dinner preparations needed to begin, the neighborhood women of the same generation would come there for a visit. They were all from the same Cheticamp to Margaree area of Cape Breton Island that Nelly emigrated from, and everyone spoke the patois French of the place. Before sitting down and settling into their seats and their mother tongue, they'd first greet me in English, then quickly switch to French.

I never understood the words they spoke to one another as they strung their patois French into sentences that sometimes made them laugh or caused them to drop half-knitted mittens or scarves into their laps and give a subject their full attention.

I felt connected to the scene on the porch, listening to the neighborhood names of Doucette, Terrio, LeBlanc, Boudrot and Aucoin —drawn to the rhythm and the resonance of the women knitting and kneading those names into their conversations and making sweet melodies in sync with the clicking of their needles.

And I've never forgotten the sounds, or lost the longing to know more about them all.

Some History

On the first of April in 1636, a group of adventurous men and women, along with a small number of children, left the west coast port of La Rochelle, France. Ninety-three passengers and crew boarded the *Saint Jehan* to brave the winds and swells of the Atlantic Ocean, traveling to La Havre, in present-day Nova Scotia, Canada.

The *Saint Jehan's* passenger list was discovered in the French *Archives Nationals*, and on the manifest, there were 70 men, 12 women, (including one widow), and 11 children on board.

The first grouping included Nicolas Le Creux, *sieur du Breuil,* along with his wife, Anne Motin. The remaining people appear to be connected to Anne—her sister Jehanne, her cousin, Jacqueline, a girl named Jehanne Billard, and Anne's two brothers, Claude and Jehan.

Also on the ship were five women traveling with their farmer husbands and nine children. The wife of a tool smith (who was accompanied by a valet) was on board with that couple's two children, and the wife of one of the master salt makers was also noted. Except for the group of people listed with Nicolas Le Creux and Anne Motin, the names of wives, children, and a servant were not given.

The 70 men were listed by name, their region of origin, and by their occupations. They were laborers, farmers, sailors, a master baker, two tailors, a cobbler, a grower of wine grapes and wine maker, a master gunsmith/locksmith, an officer of the cavalry, a master gunner, a gardener of Paris, carpenters (some were also called boat builders), and *saulniers* (those whose specialty was working the marshlands).

Since the document found is a passenger list, there's no mention of cargo, but it's interesting to wonder what else might have been on the ship—animals, tools, food, seeds, medical supplies.

Throughout the 17th century, hundreds of small European vessels, mostly Portuguese and Basque, came to the coasts of Newfoundland and the Gulf of Saint Lawrence fishing for cod. Most of them established seasonal fishing stations to clean and cure their catches, preparing them for a non-perishable return to Europe. But looking at the skills of the group traveling on the *Saint Jehan*, and the fact that they brought women and children along, it's apparent that they intended to join the permanent colony already established in Acadia.

It's not positively known why the area they were travelling to was called Acadia (*Acadie*) but it could have come from the explorer, Giovanni da Verrazzano, who used a similar word for the eastern coast of North America—meaning a pristine land in harmony with nature, and coming from the Greek ideal called *Arcadia*.

When the people arriving from France came to the area and called the land *Acadie*, they and all their descendants became known as Acadians. The early Acadians soon moved their settlement from *La Havre* to Port Royal on what is now the Annapolis River, near the Bay of Fundy, but they were not the first French settlers to choose this Fundy Basin area. In 1605, the navigator, explorer, and cartographer, Samuel de Champlain, recorded that he thought the Basin was an ideal location, believing the waters could provide anchorage for several hundred ships of the French Royal Fleet. He named the area Port Royal, and built a *Habitation* there that continued to flourish for several years. It was the first permanent European settlement north of St. Augustine, Florida.

In 1671, thirty-five years after the *Saint Jehan's* landing in *Acadie*, few of its passengers were still in Port Royal and recorded in the first Acadian census. By then, new settlers had made the voyage across the Atlantic and prospered. Their populations grew, and many of their children and grandchildren moved on from Port Royal to create new villages around the Bay of Fundy.

When they left their native France, the Acadians, who were Catholic, were not escaping religious persecution. Many historians have speculated that they were simply looking for a way to eventually own their own property and secure a better way of life.

In *Acadie*, they worked their lands and raised livestock on marshlands they drained by building dykes and *aboiteaux*. The *aboiteau* is an ingenious device that, along with the dykes, kept the salty ocean waters from the marshes during Fundy's tides (the highest in the world) and allowed fresh water to flow out to sea at low tides. After several years of the land clear of ocean water, the farmers gained marshland that was salt-free and ready for planting. Besides farming, the Acadians also hunted, fished, and trapped animals for food and fur.

The French settlers were befriended by the indigenous Mi'kmaq over the years, and the native people taught the newcomers hunting skills and the identification and use of local plants for food and medicine. The Mi'kmaq felt a kinship with the French because of their practice of diking marshes to create usable farmland, rather than the English method of deforesting the woods in order to prepare land for cultivation. The Acadians and Mi'kmag also traded with each other, to their mutual benefit.

Once their farm-ready marshes were created and native-taught hunting skills were honed, the Acadians also established commercial ties with the colonists in America and supplied the French fort at Louisbourg on *Isle Royal* (Cape Breton Island).

Acadie was a strategic commercial territory for both Britain and France, and continuing battles between the two super powers left the Acadians living alternately under French and British rule. Finally, in 1713, the Treaty of Utrecht forced France to relinquish any claims to the land, bringing the Acadians under the rule of Great Britain.

The British believed the Acadians were loyal to France and knew them to be friendly with the native Mi'kmaq, whom they considered to be dangerous savages. British officials tried to force the Acadians to sign a loyalty oath to their king, but the people of *Acadie* refused, preferring to remain neutral. After living on their lands for nearly 150 years, they no longer considered themselves French. They were Acadians wanting to live in peace, free from political warring.

The government of Britain would not accept their neutrality claims, and by 1755, they began rounding up thousands of Acadians, seizing or burning their farmlands and villages, often separating families and forcing the people onto ships. The people were scattered throughout the Atlantic seaboard or transported to France, England, the French Island of *Pierre et Michelon* off the coast of Newfoundland, and as far south as Santo Domingo. Thousands died of disease, drowning, or imprisonment

There are books written to tell of the battles, fortifications, conquests, retaliations and trauma of the Expulsion. I read many of them because I wanted to know the essential events, but tired of the details of war. Instead, I chose to look at the outcomes of these events and the impact on *my people*. What happened to the land, the women, men, and children.

The Acadians were left impoverished, without their hard-worked lands and livelihoods and set down where they were not wanted. Some escaped this fate by moving from place to place on their boats, hiding in the woods, being helped by the Mi'kmaq, or wandering and looking for refuge in order to survive.

But the Expulsion, *le Grande Dérangement,* is only a part of Acadian history. There is much more. Theirs is a rich and on-going story, and I want to explore it on the lands and paths of the people who are my ancestors.

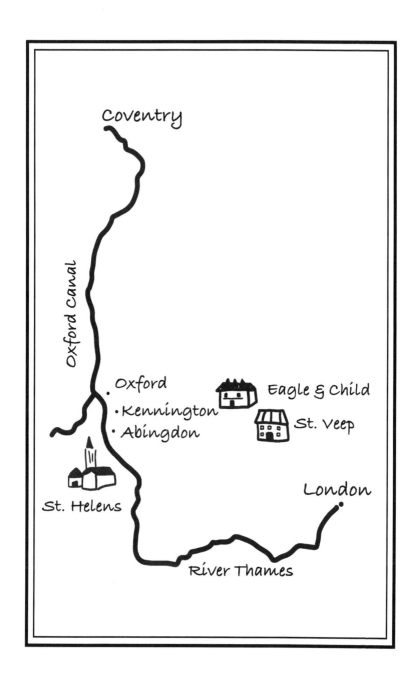

Coventry

Oxford Canal

Oxford
Kennington
Abingdon

Eagle & Child

St. Veep

St. Helens

London

River Thames

Genealogy in Cold Places

During a year's stay in England, I studied the social history and genealogy of the canal people during the Industrial Age. The class was far from any possible connection to Acadians in Nova Scotia, but it taught me how to gather information from church records, historically connect to a group of people, and situate them in time and place. What I learned there created the path that would lead me to my Acadian ancestors.

My husband was on sabbatical from his university position and our three children were attending the local schools. With the help of good English friends, we oriented ourselves and settled into a house in the small village of Kennington, nestled by the Thames River, about 6.5 miles from the town of Oxford.

We rented the main floor of a large brick Victorian house with 12-foot ceilings, a dining room to seat 10 or 12, and a kitchen you could waltz in. For reasons unknown to us, it was named after the sixth-century Cornish saint, or the Cornish parish or town named after the female *Saint Veep*. The plumbing drains ran down the outside of the old house, and inside, the rooms meandered like the famous river nearby. The place was awash with staid mahogany furniture, a grand piano, and floor-to-ceiling, theatre-weight blue velvet drapes. In the winter dusk, I was tempted to bow and tell the world *The End and Good Night* as I closed yards of velvet across the 7-foot-tall windows, and along the wooden pole over the double front doors. More than decorative (or dramatic), the curtains helped lessen the effect of the cracks around the windows and doors, and kept us reasonably draft-free and sealed off from the world.

Saint Veep's added attractions included a well-stocked library filled with British authors and a *warming cupboard* housing the hot water heater. This dandy little place also had space to finish off drying all the clothes that never completely dried outside, and had room on the floor for our fermenting bucket of homemade beer.

When the children, *Saint Veep*, and soggy clothes were somewhat sorted out, I enrolled in a non-degree course at Oxford University, studying the regional canal people. They were men and families who worked and lived on their boats while transporting cargo on the waters of the Thames and Oxford Canals. The class was research-oriented and without standard lectures. As students, our task was to collect data, and the professor taught us genealogical techniques and social history. I was eager and intrigued to try this experiential learning. Orientation featured the history and functions of England's inland waterways systems, the importance of the canals to the Industrial Revolution, and what life on the canals with cargo and the whole family on board must have been like.

When the Romans occupied Britain from AD 43 to 410, they built new canals to link rivers together for transportation and used the existing ones for irrigation. By the late 1700s, the beginning of the Industrial Revolution, the British dug more canals to meet the demand to move goods from factories to the marketplaces around the country. Existing roads were poorly constructed, often disconnected from each other, or were crude cart paths.

The railway system in Great Britain is the oldest in the world, but wasn't in operation until the 1840s, and Robert McAdam, a Scotsman, didn't develop his process for road construction (later called macadam) until around 1820. In order to serve the industrial needs of the time, expanding and improving the canals and locks appeared to be the best way to provide a safe and reliable system of transportation. This was especially true for the pottery produced in the Midlands and headed for London markets. And so the canals were further developed, and the period between the 1770s and the 1830s is often referred to as the *Golden Age of British Canals*. Early on, only men worked on the canal boats, and their families lived in cottages beside the waterways. Eventually the duties and economics of the lifestyle nudged whole families to move on to these 7-foot-wide boats. Width was determined by the maximum the bridges and locks could accommodate. The average length of a canal boat was around 50 feet and the cabins at the upper level of the boat, where whole families lived, were only 7 feet by 10 feet.

A group of our English friends went on a yearly boating holiday on the Norfolk Broads in eastern Britain, and during our year there, invited us to come along. The Broads is an area of old peat bogs, flooded over many years, connecting to rivers, and providing navigable waterways. It's not a canal with a boat's tow horse to lead, cargo to manage, or locks to work by hand, but traveling waterways on a 12- by 40-foot boat with five children aboard gave me some idea of what having a family on a canal boat must have been like.

Our little Norfolk Broad's holiday group included four boats, eight adults, and 14 children. Three of the kids on our boat were ours and two were friends visiting our children. At night, all four boats dropped anchor and were tied up within hopping distance of one another. On three of the boats, split up by age, the adults gathered on one, children with a responsible teen as chaperone on another, and the remaining teens were on the third. It was a delightful way to spend an evening, and I wondered if this was something canal boat parents might have done after a day's work.

Mid-week, somewhere in the middle of our journey, I got off our boat and walked the four miles on a water-side path into the village ahead. Alone. A sailboat, waiting for a drawbridge to lift, delayed our group back on the boat, and I arrived in the village before they did. In the slow calm of my solo outing, I sat on the river's bank hearing only soft breezes whispering, and thought about how canal boat mothers might have found any quiet times.

In the midst of all their child-minding and other work-related duties, in the Oxford class, we learned that the canal boat women found time to decorate their boats and some of the gear used in their trade. They covered many of the surfaces available with bright-colored designs of castles and roses and all varieties of geometric patterns. Even the horse's feed buckets were decorated. The women were also accomplished at complex lace crocheting and hung their creations in the cabins—turning their tiny living spaces into an art form of its own. Many a dirty coal boat's cabin was hung with delicate white lacework on its windows.

Our Oxford professor had already compiled considerable information from census records and other civil information, and we students were to do our work *in the field,* gathering data, and then coming together for a regular 3-hour class once a week. In class, we discussed our findings, shared new avenues of research, and planned future activities. I was assigned a group of names and told to gather all the information I could that was related to these people, focusing on familial relationships.

For the students, *in the field* meant in churches. Although the canal people were transient, they regularly returned to their home churches to honor and record the milestones of their lives—births, baptisms, marriages, and deaths. Often the names of godparents at the baptisms, and witnesses at marriages gave clues to family connections. Overall, the church records held a wealth of information, frustrations, and mysteries.

The list of people assigned to me were all recorded for at least one life event at *Saint Helen's Church,* built in the 13th century, and now listed as a Church of England in the market town of Abingdon. The church sits alongside the Thames and is a short drive from Kennington and *Saint Veep*.

From the beginning of our English adventure, I often shopped in Abingdon and knew this church—famous for the three sets of almshouses for the poor in the churchyard. For me, it was also memorable for its population of feral cemetery cats. I always loved walking through the graveyard on my way from the parking lot to the pedestrian blocks of shops, watching the cats, and spotting all the saucers of milk that were left beside the headstones. Clearly, these felines did not live on mice alone.

Once inside *Saint Helen's*, the helpful church secretary would disappear into some cave of a place to collect the old record books I needed for each session. She'd offer me a cup of tea, then set me up in her cozy office—the only place that was dependably heated.

After drinking my tea, I'd start diagraming all the connections and frequency of entries in *Saint Helen's* registries. It wasn't an easy task, but I enjoyed the challenge and got quite attached to *my families*. A few times, for a few weeks, I'd lose someone when I expected the person to appear in the records—actually worry about them, then cheer when they appeared again in print. It was all very strange, and sometimes I'd wonder if I was spending too much time counting dead people and cemetery cats.

I found it hard to accept the wording of births registered at the church. *Mary Ashburton, dau of William Ashburton, born on the body of Elizabeth Ashburton.* It sounded more like registering livestock. Why did William get first billing and Elizabeth was just a body (who carried baby Mary for nine months and would no doubt be the primary nurturer for a very long time)? It hadn't been that many years since I carried and delivered my own three children, so I had a definite sensitivity on this issue. In class, I raised a question about the wording on birth registries and from the professor's answer we all learned a lot about the history and laws regarding children whose fathers were not revealed. Church parishes, as well as civil offices were very concerned about paternity at this time. They wanted to know who would be supporting a child, so they wouldn't have to. There were also issues of inheritance and the passage of land through families. It's been mentioned that if the mother was unwed, midwives were instructed to try and get the woman to name the father while she was in the throes of labor!

Weekly class meetings were held in what felt like the coldest classroom in the British Isles. We shivered our way through the sharing of information and discussions of our findings while learning social/anthropological history and planning future directions. Once class was over for the week, the next stop was always the local pub. We were all hungry and cold.

The public house is a British institution — a meeting place for friends and family, a destination for a game of darts, or the focal point of a community. Our *local*, a natural destination, was just a few blocks from class. *The Eagle and Child*, fondly known as *The Bird and Baby* (and even *The Fowl and Foetus*) is named for the story of a noble-born baby found in an eagle's nest. It was the favorite pub of writers C.S Lewis and J.R.R. Tolkien. History tells us that they spent most of their time in the *Rabbit Room*, a private lounge at the back of the building.

Our small, chilled class preferred the main room, in front of the mammoth fireplace with a roaring fire — as close to it as possible. *The Bird and Baby* always offered a standard Ploughman's Lunch of cheese (The *Manchester*

Guardian recommends *three hard or semi-hard BRITISH cheeses of contrasting flavours and textures served at room temperature* as ideal. At *The Bird and Baby*, there was always at least one cheddar and two other varieties that went along with it. The bread was crusty and rustic, and there was always a pickle. The pickle in a Ploughman's is not a North American style cucumber pickle. It's a little closer to a chutney and in most places, if not home-made, it was probably *Branson's*.

Our class always ordered in unity. The Ploughman's and a half-pint of dark, room temperature, *Guinness Stout*. Just now, as I look on the web to find the actual degrees of room temperature, the *Guinness* website is the only one I've ever visited that has required me to give my date of birth before letting me in. Because, they state, they believe in responsible drinking. *Guinness* answered many questions about their brew, but none about desired serving temperatures. Other sites, though, called room temperature ideal and said it was 42 degrees Fahrenheit.

Each week, after getting thawed out by the fire and nourished by the Ploughman's with a hearty Irish stout served at the appropriate temperature, I'd hop the bus home to *Saint Veep* and store my class notes in a box earmarked to travel with us on our return back across the Atlantic, where I could use them again.

Not Much to Go On

Departing England and returning home was a combination of delight and culture shock. Everything in America seemed large, open, and loud. The small British lorries were replaced with 18-wheelers on enormous highways. All the restaurants had televisions playing, people engaged in boisterous conversations, and overly friendly wait-staff who wanted to tell me their names and that they'd be my server—instead of just calling me *Dear* and asking if I wanted a cup of tea.

I would clearly have to acclimate my nervous system in order to survive.

On the other hand, it was our home. All the neighborhood children rushed to the house to welcome us back. Their parents arrived with food, and one came with clean fluffy towels—the kind that would take a week to dry in England. Friends called or dropped by to visit and get our news. Our kids quickly dropped their British accents and changed into jeans. The cat, who'd stayed with the renters, swatted me on my outreached arm, then forgave me and climbed on my lap. I fell into the busy routine of being back, but opened a desk drawer and put my genealogy notes in a prominent place as soon as I unpacked them.

When I spoke to my father, I told him I was ready to start looking into the lives of his Nova Scotian parents and our Acadian ancestors.

"I've learned how to begin the process," I told him.

"I'll write down everything I know about them," he said. "And bring all the information with us when Mom and I come to visit."

A few weeks later, they arrived, and after all the usual hugging and settling in for their stay, I had some quiet time with my father. Before long, he brought up the subject of the Acadian relatives, reached into his pocket, then handed me a folded piece of yellow graph paper and said, "I wrote down everything I know about the Cape Breton relatives. I'm thinking that since you researched all those British canal boat people, doing our family genealogy should be easy. I'm really curious about these ancestors. They're the people nobody ever talked about."

"If nobody ever talked about them, are there strange and weird things I should be looking for?" I teased. He went on to explain that his parents spoke French to each other and English to the five children. "They never taught us any French. This seemed to be the norm in our neighborhood," he said. "None of the Landry or Doucette kids spoke much or any French either. Fred and Nelly could have been talking to one another about relatives, but they didn't share any of it with us. I don't blame them," he added. "Ours was a busy household, Cape Breton was a long way from Newton, Massachusetts, and there was no extra money for travel to meet relatives. Like most immigrant families, they also wanted their children to be like all their peers in the country where they lived."

I felt the loss that spoken French had not been passed on to all of us, then remembered that my oldest cousin, who grew up in the Faxon Street house, was told by the nuns at school not to speak the French they heard at home—that it wasn't *good* French. They were referring to the patois French that dominated the neighborhood.

I told my father that it might take a while, but I'd gladly do the genealogy research for him—and for myself and my children. I said that I'd love to know more about our heritage, then to pass the knowledge on. And how fortunate for me that Cape Breton is such a beautiful place to wander around in.

While he gave me a satisfied sigh, I unfolded the paper he'd prepared and met my challenge head-on. My father was a methodical man. Letters and lists from him were usually ordered and precise. This one was different. It was covered in his strong, efficient handwriting, but with tiny shards of information, and a heavy sprinkling of question marks, erasures, and repetitions spread randomly across the page.

*Arichat, Petit de Grat, Cape Breton, Isle Madame, Margaree, someone was a boat captain, Frederick Boudrot, Nelly Burns, Was Uncle Willie really an uncle?, Gaeton Boudrot—a grandfather I never met, my cousin Mae—that's where you got your middle name—*and in my mother's high-strung writing—*Agathe Ryan, Nelly's mother from Friar's Head.*

There were dates of deaths with some of the names, but no birth years on any of them. "Not much to go on," I said, and with half a grin and a nod, my father agreed.

The places on the yellow paper were all familiar. I had explored them in earlier years—even the lesser-known *Cap le Moine* (Friar's Head) with its eye-catching shape and name. This grass-covered mound of earth, shaped like a religious cap, sits on the ocean side of the road on the way to Cheticamp, and is easy to spot. On my first visits to the Island, I had no specific goals. Now, since my assignment, I was eager to return to beautiful, quirky, Cape

Breton again — this time with a definite purpose. I'd be looking for *my people's* places and all the information I could find about them.

In order to get started from my home in Pennsylvania, I made a sketchy genealogical plan. Beginning with my grandparents, Nelly and Frederick Boudrot, I could do census work online, and because of the time I'd spent searching old records at *St. Helen's* in England (the one with the almshouses and all the graveyard cats), it was natural for me to do a family search in a church.

My grandparents belonged to the Catholic parish of *Saint Jean l'Evangeliste* in Newton, Massachusetts. *Saint Jean's* had closed, but *Our Lady Help of Christians,* in the same city, had *Saint Jean's* records, and provided me with all the information that I asked for. After preliminary calls and letters, the good people at *Our Lady's* sent copies of documents related to marriages, which included names of parents, with some dates, and other clues, such as names of godparents and witnesses at weddings. I also collected information on my father and his siblings and was now minimally ready to go ancestor hunting.

Checking Massachusetts census records, I found that the enumeration from 1930 gave an abundance of information. Frederick Boudrot reported that he was 61 years old (born in 1869), in French Canada, and when he was 16, in 1885, he immigrated to the United States. He also reported that he was a naturalized citizen. Nelly Burns, his wife, is identified on the same 1930 census as 56 years old, an *alien*, born in 1873, in French Canada and immigrated to the United States in 1898.

They both listed French as their preferred language, but said they also spoke English. Fred could read and write, but Nelly could not. My cousin, who lived with Nelly for a while, said he signed all his parental permission and excuse slips from school—and got away with a few minor escapades in the process. Both Nelly and Fred said they had not gone to school. They owned their own home and reported that it was worth $6,000. (On the internet today, the house's estimated value is nearly a million dollars, its 2940 square feet is divided into two housing units, and the basement is still unfinished. The site reports that the house was built in 1900.)

Fred died before I was born, and I was 11 years old when Nellie died. Her illiteracy never surfaced in our relationship. Who needs to read and write in order to give affection and knit mittens with cuffs that go half way up a child's arms to keep out the snow? And to make bread whose smell encircled a small child and tasted like pure love.

I continued to search as many census documents as I could find, and all of them were in agreement regarding Nelly and Fred's data. Each enumeration year only differed in numbers of questions asked, members of the household added or removed, and the changes to each person's age. My next task was to read enough Cape Breton history and geography to prepare for future searches on genealogical trips. In our family, *Red Rose* is considered to be the best Canadian tea, and during all of my reading, I sipped my way through many cups of it. The tea was made from the multiple packages I always brought from Canada to Pennsylvania. (Red Rose is sold in the U.S., but the American variety is weaker and doesn't come in individual *gauze* bags.)

.

The Cape Breton Island my grandparents left was remote. Roads were few, and the terrain was difficult. It was almost impossible to travel across the highlands of the Island until the 1930s, long after my grandparents left. The distance from Cheticamp (near Nelly's childhood home) to Pleasant Bay is 24 miles, over some of the most rugged terrain in eastern North America, and wasn't paved until 1962. Before that, most people traveled by water, if they traveled at all. Until 1955, traveling by boat was the only way to cross the 65 meter (213 feet) deep Strait of Canso to get to mainland Nova Scotia from Cape Breton. Until the 1700s, the Island was mostly inhabited by Mi'kmaq natives. The word *Canso* is thought to come from the Mi'kmaq word *komsak*, meaning *opposite the lofty cliffs*. Within the Island's more than 10,000 square kilometers (about 4000 square miles) there are plenty of cliffs reaching down to the sea.

Once, in the fog, I drove on the Cabot Trail around the Island's rugged northern highlands with my Australian Shepherd dog as an only companion. On this trip, the visibility was so low that I couldn't see the shear drops from the road to the sea below. But because I'd traveled the route before, I knew they were there. Chugging up the twisting mountain road from sea level to frightening heights, eyes glued to the parts of the road I could actually see, with shaking voice, I called to my dog in his backseat nest, **"These are more than lofty cliffs!"** He stood up and pushed his muzzle into my cheek in solidarity, but I didn't dare lift my hands off the steering wheel to give him a grateful pat.

Our early ancestors came to Cape Breton after the British expelled the Acadians from their lands in 1755. This event is heart wrenching to delve into. My ancestors lost their homes, but they were fortunate to escape the deportation that befell thousands of their fellow Acadians. Four generations before the birth of my grandmother, Nelly, her maternal ancestor, Apolline Arseneau went to Cape Breton when it was called *Isle Royale* and under French control. Her family had escaped capture by the British and traveled from place to place to find safety and sustenance. Once she arrived on *Isle Royal*, Apolline remained there for the rest of her life. All of the other women in my matrilineal line, and their families, remained in Cape Breton—until Nelly. She was the first to leave the Island.

Cape Breton became a part of Nova Scotia in 1763, but remained sparsely developed by European arrivals until 1784, when it was designated a separate colony and given unique jurisdiction for Loyalists—those who sided with the British in the American Revolution. There was also a wave of Scottish immigrants after the Highland Clearances in Scotland, and before that, an influx of Irish. In 1955, a causeway was opened across the deep waters of the Canso Strait, connecting Cape Breton Island to mainland Nova Scotia. Newspapers of the day reported that 40,000 people showed up for the grand opening of this monumental connector, and 400 bagpipers piped their way across it. The mind boggles (and my ears hurt) just thinking about 400 bagpipers in one place. Personally, I like a soulful, kilted piper playing in the distance, facing the ocean. I say this with great apologies to my maternal grandfather, Duncan MacDonald Lorimer, and all those Scottish ancestors who came before him. Duncan's ancestors came to mainland Nova Scotia from the borderlands of Scotland, while the first Scots in Cape Breton came from the country's Highlands. Today there's a lively mix of people on the Island, with great ethnic pride among the groups, and fierce loyalty to being a Cape Bretoner.

A friend of mine tells of attending University on mainland Nova Scotia when a professor in one of her classes began a role call to find out where all the students were from. When he asked for a show of hands from the people who were from somewhere other than Nova Scotia, a whole enclave of Cape Bretoners raised their hands along with the others from away.

When the professor called on the Cape Breton students, the first one said she was from Cape Breton Island.

"Come on," the professor said. "That's a part of Nova Scotia."

"It's Cape Breton," they all answered, and while keeping their hands high in the air, steadfastly added, "It's Cape Breton Island— and always will be."

But I knew so little of so much of all of this on the day my father handed me his sketchy notes on a piece of yellow graph paper and joined me in yearning to know more about our Cape Breton roots.

Like Trees Swaying in the Breeze

On all my early visits to Cape Breton, I always scanned the passing faces for potential relatives, hoping to discover someone who looked like my father's family, or maybe me. I've painted some portraits, and often catch myself staring at earlobes or the space between a person's lips and nose—the small details that matter when you're trying to capture an image. On these trips, though,

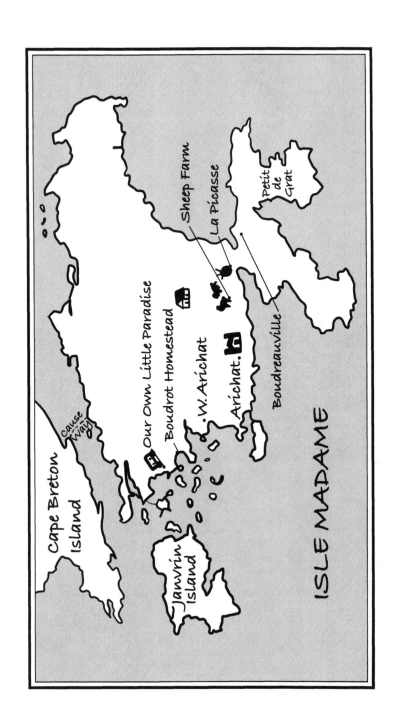

Cape Breton Island

Cause Way

Janvrin Island

Our Own Little Paradise

Boudrot Homestead

.W. Arichat

Arichat.

Sheep Farm

La Picasse

Petit de Grat

Boudreauville

ISLE MADAME

I was looking at the whole face for a familiar family look.

In the churchyard in Arichat on Isle Madame, Cape Breton Island, the assumed birthplace of my grandfather, and first location on my father's list, I found what I was looking for.

The *Notre Dame d'Assomption* church is the most majestic structure in the area. Its cemetery side sits on a slope sliding down to the sea. The old white wooden church has two bell towers rising high on each side of its main door, which was slightly open on the day of my visit, so I wandered through. Inside, the enormous painting of Mary ascending into heaven fills much of the wall behind the altar. I stopped to view the dramatic scene—Mary with outstretched arms, looking upward and surrounded by cherubs holding a pillow-like cloud. Her robe is dark blue, and she's wearing a soft red dress. I found it soulful, meditative.

Moving beyond the painting, I quieted my steps among the statues, even though there was no one around. Across the way, there was the familiar smell of wax burning, and I slid

among the pews over to the wrought iron bank
of tapers, to put some money in the metal box
and light candles for Nelly and Fred. Nearby
stairs led up to a gallery that reached around
three sides of the building, and at the back was
an old pipe organ, marked *Philadelphia* in bold
print above the keyboard. I found later that it is
one of three in existence and was converted to
electric bellows in 1956. A framed note hanging
on a pillar downstairs also explained that the
building is a combination of Neo-Classical and
Gothic-Revival architecture and is the oldest
surviving Roman Catholic Church in Nova
Scotia. The altar painting of Mary, it told, was
brought from Rome.

While I stood reading, the front door
creaked open, and a man who looked more like
a tourist than a priest came in, crossed himself
and stopped to take in the surroundings. As
he moved along one wall looking at the art, I
walked over to ask if he knew how to find the
priest. I explained that I was researching my
Boudrot ancestry and wanted to look at some
church records. He said he'd seen a sign for the

glebe house across the road, then asked if I'd step outside to meet his wife who was in the cemetery looking for Boudrot headstones.

After leaving the church, we wove our way through the oldest section of the graveyard, the part with the best view of the sea. In a far corner, the man's wife was balancing herself on uneven ground, trying to decipher old moss-laden letters on a tipsy gravestone. She pulled herself upright in greeting, and when we took a good look at each other, we both gasped. Her husband laughed—because he'd anticipated what would happen when we met.

"You look more like my daughter than my daughter does," she said.

"And you," I told her, "look more like my mother than my mother does."

Both of our fathers were Boudrots. She was a genealogical newcomer from Ontario with as few clues about her family as I had about mine. Sadly, the little information we each had was of no value to the other. So, we parted, still astonished by how alike we looked, and how far we'd have to go to put together a family tree. If this happened today, I would reach for my cell phone and take a picture: *Two Look-alike,*

Novice Boudrot-Seekers Standing in a Cemetery by the Sea. But on that day, my bulky camera was hanging around my husband's neck somewhere on the Arichat shoreline.

Now, I think of this chance meeting, and am surprised that I didn't ask for the woman's name and address. I also wonder if my mirror mother ever found her Boudrot family, as I did mine—and how closely were we related? But on that day in the Arichat cemetery, I was too obsessed with finding records, I guess.

When I crossed the road to the glebe house, the young priest who answered the door reached out his hand in greeting, invited me inside, and offered to help. A quick search of *Notre Dame d'Assomption's* registries produced no results for Frederick Boudrot, and the priest's disappointment seemed equal to mine. I thanked him for his effort, and he volunteered to continue looking for Frederick, saying the winter nights were long in Nova Scotia, and he always enjoyed some good genealogical searches to keep him occupied. In April, I received a letter from him saying he'd searched everywhere he could think of and found nothing. By summer, I found the reason why—it was the wrong church. My people belonged to the *West* Arichat parish, and in 1882, a fire burned that church and all their records. I would have to find other methods to search for Frederick, his father Gaeton, and his mother, Adelle LeBlanc, whom I'd learned about from Frederick and Nelly's church wedding records in Newton.

For quite awhile, my research languished, but in the Spring of 2004, I decided to go back to Arichat on Isle Madame. As I drove over the second causeway, I thought; *My grandfather lived on an island off Cape Breton Island, off mainland Nova Scotia— two water crossings just to get to mainland Nova Scotia.* When he left in 1885, he probably traveled more directly from Arichat to Boston by ship, as Arichat, with its deep harbor and ship building capabilities, was on its way to becoming a busy port.

My plan this time was to have a week to seriously explore the Arichat area and get back to ancestor-searching. All things Acadian were in the air in Maritime Canada that year. The large Acadian Congress starting on August 15th, *National Acadian Day*, was being planned, and Nova Scotia was hosting the celebration. I packed up some books, my notes, computer, spinning wheel and fleece and checked into *L'Auberge Acadienne*, a charming inn that sits on a rise parallel to the sea.

Isle Madame is roughly 7 miles wide, 10 miles long, and dotted with sturdy evergreens and rocky outcroppings by the ocean. The Inn was easy to find on one of Arichat's two main roads in this town of 2000. At the beginning of my stay, I mostly drove around the area, going through *Boudreauville* onto Boudreau Road and Boudreau Lane. How odd for a woman who spent her early years always spelling her last name and correcting its pronunciation to be in a land where the names Boudrot and Boudreau were so common. It's a mystery when Boudrot, the spelling the original Acadians arrived with, was changed to Boudreau. But my grandfather was an *o-t* Boudrot when he arrived in Massachusetts in 1885, and there has never been a change of spelling in our family.

I kept the local French radio station on in the car as I drove around the island from *Arichat* to *West Arichat, D'Escousse, Martinique, Poirierville, Cap La Ronde, Petit-de-Grat, Ponduille* and *Boudreauville* — taking in the beautiful scenery and trying to remember some high school French. To my untrained ear, the words I heard were sometimes understandable, but the pronunciation was different from the French I'd studied and later heard in France. Scholars say some of the language spoken in Acadian areas is the oldest French spoken anywhere. It's the French brought to Canada by its earliest settlers.

At *Petit-de-Grat*, I stopped at *La Picasse*, the Francophone cultural center. A replica of a wood, rock, and rope anchor called *la picasse*, stands near the front door. What a perfect name for a town center housing the local historical society, library, cafe, and a large multi-purpose area, I thought — the anchor. Inside, there were people milling around, but the Genealogy Center hadn't opened yet, so I bought a cup of coffee and sat down in the cafe. Like most Acadians I'd met in other places, the local people spoke English in addition to French, so it was easy for me to get involved in multiple conversations. The people were curious and friendly, and it wasn't very long before I was invited to the potluck dinner to be held in the multi-purpose room that evening. "Don't bring any food," they said. "There's always too much at these dinners."

That night, a couple I'd met having morning coffee at *La Picasse* picked me up at the Inn and brought me to the event. They were right about the food. There was more than enough! Seafood, potatoes and an assortment of homemade pies were in abundance.

We sat at one of many large round tables and as the word got passed around to others nearby that I was from *away* and on *Isle Madame* looking for my Boudrot relatives, people started trying to figure out who I looked like, and might be related to. They made a guessing game out of it, and I scanned the room—looking for potentials to point out, but found none.

While this was going on, many of the men and women started moving chairs and lining them up in two long straight lines. Each of the line of chairs faced the other, with a 6-foot gap in between. The women sat on one side, the men on the other.

In French, the men and women first sang in unison. Then, on the following melodies, the men sang to the women and the women responded in song. There was an easy, beautiful harmony to the whole exchange. Like trees swaying back and forth in the breeze.

At Christmas, Come on up to the House

My week's stay in Arichat, on Isle Madame, Cape Breton, was three months before the 2004 *Acadian World Congress*, which was scheduled to include family reunions spread around the province of Nova Scotia. These gatherings take place every five years, with Opening Day events in one location, and on the following days, people travel to designated towns to focus exclusively on their own families.

Over 100 reunions scattered across Nova Scotia were planned for 2004, and Arichat was where the Boudrots (and all the variations of the name) would be gathering.

I wanted to get a head-start finding some ancestors before the August event, with all those Boudrots coming to attend the reunion. Since I had such a flimsy foundation of facts to build on, I imagined I'd need a long period of genealogy searching to discover much of anything. The news of the burned West Arichat church and its records had left me floundering, and scouring Arichat census records turned out to be nonproductive. I had so few dates and there were too many Boudrots with too many repetitions of first names.

In Arichat, pre-reunion anticipation filled the air. Everywhere I went, people were welcoming and helpful. During the night of singing and dancing at *La Picasse*, many of them encouraged me to go back to the Genealogy Center and get the help I needed to begin the process of finding all *my* Boudrots. The next morning, I went to the Center, bringing my meager little notebook filled with what Boudrot information I'd found so far. And for good measure and good luck, I put my father's list—the one on the folded yellow paper, in my pocket.

Inside a small room beside the cafe, Josette Boudreau Marchant, the Arichat reunion organizer, greeted me warmly, and asked what my father's name was.

"Oh," I said, "I have more information than that," extending my notebook in her direction.

"I only need your father's name," she said. "The government genealogists just finished researching the Boudrot family; after the LeBlancs, it's one of the largest of all Acadian families."

I tucked my notebook back under my arm and waited while she entered my father's name into the computer—quietly pushing keys until the printer came alive and started delivering paper onto its tray. Josette gave me a smile that lit up her whole face, and said she thought I'd be pleased, as we both watched the pages print. When the machine went silent, there in print were nine generations of *my* Boudrots, going back to Michel, born around 1601 in France, who married Michelle Aucoin and arrived in *Acadie*.

I felt like I'd struck it rich. The list was so tidy and complete. A genealogical gold mine. Names and dates, husbands and wives, and a whole social history to explore. Where did they live? How did they survive the Expulsion? Where did they go before somebody came to Isle Madame? These questions rolled around in my brain, and in the middle of my amazement and joy, it was clear how much reading and further researching there was for me to do. I could hardly wait to get started. I had nine husbands and wives to trace. How many Acadian settlements to discover? A genealogical bonanza delivered by a printer at *La Picasse*.

I stayed in Arichat another day or two, and before leaving Isle Madame, I was put on the roster to demonstrate hand carding and spinning during the upcoming summer reunion. I was involved in fiber art at the time, spinning raw fleece from the sheep of Atlantic Canada into yarn to use in my fiber projects—

and that fit in nicely with the arts and crafts section of upcoming reunion events.

MacAusland's Woolen Mill on Prince Edward Island was the source of all my raw fleece. Well known for their high quality 100% woolen blankets, the business started out as a sawmill and roll mill in 1870. In 1902, they began producing yarn, and in 1932, blankets. The production area in their western island location hums with machines spinning in full roar, and the wool washing space churns with soap and water—cleaning very dirty wool recently shorn off Maritime sheep. Upstairs in the sales room, the staff was continuously helpful to a hand spinner, allowing me to go into a storage space and crawl around on the floor, diving into a hill of off–white minimally processed fleece, looking for the best I could find. While on my hands and knees, I always hoped I wouldn't scoop up a mouse in the process. Luckily, I never encountered one and came home each time with tall bags of fleece to spin.

I had a substantial stash of PEI fleece at home, but wondered if there were any sheep on Isle Madame. It felt more authentic to demonstrate spinning with local fleece. I was told there was a great sheep farm nearby, and going there to get the promised fleece provided an entertaining hour in an Arichat barn. The shearer had just been to the farm and the owner shared some of the cleanest cuttings with me.

I also met the farm owner's mother, who immigrated to Nova Scotia from England years earlier. When my children were young, and we lived in England, we loved to watch the television series, *All Creatures Great and Small,* based on the practice of the Yorkshire vet, James Herriot (real name, Alf Wight). On one of the last episodes, a young vet left Herriot's practice and moved to Nova Scotia to teach at an agricultural college. With my Canadian connections, my ears perked up hearing the Nova Scotia reference, and I remembered that episode. Now, many years later, I found myself in a barn in Arichat with the real life wife of the *All Creatures Great and Small* vet who left Yorkshire for Canada.

With fleece and my newly acquired ancestral chart, I returned home and started researching and reaching out to learn more about the Acadians and their place in history. I joined *Ancestry.ca* and looked up the Boudrot names in my ancestral line. There were a lot of people doing Acadian ancestry online and also some excellent websites devoted to the subject. I joined a Boudrot (and the variations of the name) family group, communicated with a Boudrot in Louisiana, and most importantly traveled to the *Université de Moncton* in New Brunswick, to meet with the pre-eminent Acadian genealogy scholar, Stephen White.

It was a stroke of synchronicity that Stephen White's father and my father graduated from the same high school in the same year. His grandparents lived in the neighborhood in Newton, Massachusetts where mine had, which gave us reminiscences in common about our French grandparents and their homes. We'd walked the same streets and visited the same landmarks as children, and Stephen also had ancestors who came from Arichat.

At this time, I was too unschooled in genealogy to take full advantage of Stephen's knowledge or to access the incredible library references at the Acadian Center—that would come later, when I knew enough to ask some worthwhile questions. It was also at this point that I started to realize that most genealogists have a skill I was lacking—the ability to memorize names, dates, places, and keep multi-generations neatly organized in their minds. "It's only nine generations," I told myself. Surely I should be able to remember the vital statistics of nine people. But I was always adding more places, ancestors and anecdotes, jumbling the Simons and Prosperes and a Francois with a Francoise.

Out of frustration, I sat down with all my data, a blank index card and black pen, and wrote the names, dates, spouses (making it 18 names) of my nine generations of Boudrots, covering the front and back of the card. Then

I laminated it, punched a hole at the top and strung it with a long leather cord. When the cord was secured, I hung the whole thing around my neck and felt amazingly complete and powerful. I was ready to answer any questions about my heritage—ready to attend the Boudrot Reunion. Still, when August came, I was excited but nervous.

After packing the car and our small Casita trailer with everything we thought we'd need, my husband and I drove our two dogs to the kennel where we always boarded them. I handed the dogs, along with all their food and supplements, to the woman in charge. She'd been in the business of keeping dogs for years, and when I gave her a vial of *Rescue Remedy* (a natural herbal for anxiety), in case the dogs needed it, she smiled and gave it back to me. "You keep it," she said. "You look like you'll need it more than the dogs."

The drive from the kennel (near Pugwash) to Arichat was about a 3-hour trip along the shore of the Northumberland Strait, until we turned inland and joined up with the TransCanada highway. The scenery that day was windswept, green, and beautifully calm. Arriving at the place where we could see Cape Breton, as in every other crossing of the Canso Causeway, I settled into a mellow and happy state of mind. Cape Breton always felt like *home*.

Because we had a few offers from people in Arichat to park our trailer in their driveway during the festivities, our housing was taken care of. We arrived a day early to give ourselves some time to wander and get oriented, before settling on somebody's pavement. When we leisurely entered Isle Madame and turned off onto a small peninsula, the sun was sparkling on the dancing ocean and the whole scene was so inviting that we pulled off the road on the water's edge and made a picnic to take out on the grass.

After we ate by the sea and were ready to move on, a car drove up slowly and stopped beside us.

"Oh, no," I said. "Are we on your property? We just finished eating and are about to go."

"Yes," the man said. "It's our little paradise. Enjoy yourselves and stay as long as you like, but at Christmas, come on up to the house!"

The next morning, his wife walked down their long driveway to invite us to dinner, and we ended up spending the whole reunion weekend by the sea, sharing their *paradise*.

There were over 500 people at the official Boudrot festivities, carrying the name in all its many variations from Boudrot to the least known Budrow. Most distant travelers came from eastern Canada and Quebec, others from many parts of the U.S—especially New England and Louisiana. Some traveled from the central coastland of France—where all the original Acadians departed their homeland in the 1600s.

While I was busy demonstrating spinning, my husband was occupied with buying books and checking lineage charts. The walls of a gymnasium were covered with large genealogical diagrams of the Boudrot family, starting with Michel, born around 1600, and his wife Michelle Aucoin, born around 1622—both in France. All of their children were listed on the gym walls — from their daughter Francoise, to their eighth child, a son, Francois born in 1666. My line branches off through Francois. When I finished spinning, my husband and I walked our way through my lineage, wall chart by wall chart.

The laminated card, with all the Boudrot information hanging around my neck, proved repeatedly useful while I was talking with others. Conversations always skipped over Michel Boudrot and Michelle Aucoin. We all descended from them. They would usually start with, "Do you have a Francois?"

"Yes, I do."

"How about Joseph?" I'd reach down, take hold of the laminated card, turn it to double check, then verify.

"Yes, I have a Joseph, married to Marguerite Dugas. Born in 1692."

Many of the first names were so frequently used, that it was important to have spouses and dates. Still holding my card in reading position, I'd ask, "Louis? Do you have Louis next?"

"No, I have _____ in that generation. "

It was like a nine generation game of *Bingo* or *Go Fish*. Never getting all the way to a win, but always ending with an, "Oh, too bad, but we're still cousins!"

I eventually did get introduced to a more direct cousin. My grandfather's youngest sister was the only member of that family who never left Isle Madame. Her granddaughter, my second cousin, was still there, living in *Petit de Grat*. She was a retired nurse and had medical questions she wanted to ask me. It turns out that some of the issues that ran in her family did not run in mine, and I was of no help to her in this area. But we enjoyed a pleasant visit at their home and stayed in contact. She knew that all of her grandmother's family had gone to *the Boston States*, but that's all she had ever heard about any of us.

My husband, who's from Kansas, found a connection at the Boudrot Reunion. While I was spinning, a young college student lingered, asking lots of questions. After a while she said, "I have to go get my mother (a Budrow), she's a weaver and will love seeing the wheel and you spinning."

When she came back with her mother, I asked the mother-daughter duo where they were from. It was Laramie, Wyoming.

"My husband has two aunts who live in Laramie," I told them, and when they asked who they were, I said, "Lucile Tihen and Regina Barrington."

"Regina Barrington!" the college student said. "She's my godmother!"

Throughout the rest of the reunion, we glided our way through tours, musical presentations, dances, and multiple conversations until it was time to go back to our friendly *landlord's paradise*, pack up our trailer, purchased books, ancestry charts, souvenirs, and leave.

On the way out of Arichat, we stopped to get gas and in the bay next to ours, a man was finishing fueling his car. I didn't notice him at first, but when I looked over, our eyes met and

I held my breath. It was my deceased father, or a carbon copy of him. He smiled at me and I called out the window, "Are you a Boudrot?" "Oh, yes," he said. Then drove away.

The Mother Line

O n one of the afternoons of the Boudrot
Reunion in Arichat, we left our little
Casita parked by the water's edge and drove two
hours west across Cape Breton, then north to
Cheticamp. This Acadian-centered town is on
the western, Northumberland Strait side of the
Island—on the Cabot Trail and at the gateway
to the Cape Breton Highlands National Park.
It's an area of raw and spectacular beauty.

During the Boudrot Reunion in Arichat,
I found that my grandmother, Nelly, had an

Aucoin grandmother. At the same time the Boudrots were in Arichat, the Aucoin family was gathering for their reunion in Cheticamp, so I decided to go up there and meet some Aucoins.

Driving into Cheticamp, filled with visiting Aucoins, a host of *Bienvenue/Welcome* signs greeted us everywhere we looked. Aucoin banners peppered front lawns, and multitudes of Acadian flags lined the main street that follows the harbor its entire way. This town, like Arichat, was ready to party, and there were obviously many people already celebrating. It was difficult to find a place to park, and as we drove the main street of town, cars were lined along both sides and there were *Complet/ NoVacancy* signs on every motel and bed and breakfast in sight. Fortunately for us, our little travel trailer was sitting on its spot of *paradise* back in Arichat, waiting for our late night return. When we finally found somewhere to park, it was a long walk getting to the Aucoin gathering place, giving me plenty of time to feel unprepared before going into the large arena where they were meeting.

I had no Aucoin ancestor laminated card hanging around my neck. There weren't any Aucoins in Cheticamp I'd visited with. No one I'd eaten with at a pot-luck or watched as they danced and sang, as I had in Arichat. The Aucoins were only a small part of my grandmother's heritage, and since I knew nothing about them, I began to wonder if I should even be at their reunion. Until I felt a gentle shove from Nelly, reminding me that she was the reason I was there. I wanted to know not just the place she came from, but also her people. And the Aucoins, some of her people, were just inside the door.

As soon as we walked into the large gathering place, a smiling woman wearing the colors of the Acadian flag and an official greeting tag came towards us. She was so welcoming I wanted to give her a hug, but didn't. After the greeting, she asked which of the two Aucoin brothers we were descended from, and my husband swooped his hand over to point at me, then stepped back—leaving me to say that I didn't know. Every question she asked, I had to answer with the same, "I don't know." I mumbled something about being sorry that I knew so little, and she continued trying to fit me in somewhere, so she could do her job and send me to the part of the hall where my direct-line information was.

When nothing she asked, and none of my answers seemed to be leading anywhere, she took hold of my hand with both of hers, and in the kindest voice, told me not to worry, that if there was an Aucoin in my family tree, we were cousins of some sort, and I was most welcome here.

"Come right on in," she said.

We then signed in and spent a couple of hours wandering around and looking at the large lineage charts on the wall. But no matter how full and well prepared charts are, they provide few clues when you start with as little information as I had.

The people we chatted with were warm and welcoming, and I felt content to be a tiny part of them. A woman behind a desk told me of the variations of their family name. One was O'Quin—the name of one of Nelly's neighbors. No wonder the French Mrs. O'Quin spoke sounded just like all the other women on Nelly's porch.

On that day in Cheticamp with all the Aucoins, I resolved to learn more about my grandmother's heritage. She was my favorite grandparent, and I knew so little about her. Right there, in Cheticamp, I committed to researching the matrilineal line—the mother line. Starting with Nelly, I wanted to know her mother, and maternal grandmother and all the women connected to her back to the first of her female ancestors who came from France to *Acadie* in the 1600s.

So far, my experience with genealogy had always focused on following the male line through one family name. This time, I would set out to know all of my Acadian foremothers— mother to mother to mother.

It Was a Gift, a Heritage of Names

After the Boudrot Reunion, I filed all the information I'd been given and propped the laminated card of names and dates against some family photos. The card had served me well.

In a few weeks, I felt more committed than ever to go back to Cape Breton—this time to the Cheticamp region, to begin the search for Nelly's ancestral mothers. I'd been there many times before, but only once with ancestors in mind.

The town of Cheticamp, on the Cabot Trail outside the Cape Breton Highlands National Park, is a well-known center of Acadian culture. The Trail, the Park, and the town are all popular tourist destinations. The area is rich in ocean views and houses with colors and roofs that have a jaunty look. Like all the other nearby fishing villages, Cheticamp was isolated before the completion of the Cabot Trail in 1932.

The Trail is a nearly 300-km (186-mile) loop of spectacular scenery that spans the top half of Cape Breton, from the Gulf of Saint Lawrence's Northumberland Strait to the Atlantic Ocean. Or the other way around. It depends on whether you choose to drive clockwise or counterclockwise. I always go clockwise, because in that direction the driver is on the inside of the road, not on the edge of the cliffs.

It was on the trip I took with my dog in the fog over the *lofty cliffs* when I first scouted the area to find out about Acadians in the region. I stopped at the renowned Margaree River for a look at the salmon pools, then drove over to Cheticamp Island to let Baxter have a run. This dog always loved the water's edge—the beach at low tide or the marsh at any time. On Cheticamp Island, I let him out on the shore to give him a good romp before he needed to stay in the car while I explored some places on my own.

Our timing was perfect. The tide was going out and Baxter was always wildly excited to sniff his way along the high-tide mark to find the treasures the receding ocean left on the shore. He was a 65-pound Australian Shepherd, ruggedly handsome and athletic, but he wore himself out smelling seaweed and dead crabs and chasing seagulls to the water's edge, until, squawking angrily, they'd fly away.

After his adventures, Baxter was settling into sleep as I lowered the car windows to give him some cool sea air outside *La Co-operative Artisanale* (The Craft Cooperative) on the edge of town. The temperature was in the sixties and when I looked at the sea, I sensed a storm working its way across the Northumberland Strait.

La Co-operative Artisanale is no longer in operation, but on this day, it was busy, and the smells from the restaurant's kitchen reached me with the message that it was time to eat. Their specialty was Acadian food served by women in the old-style Acadian dress of long skirts, aprons, and a kind of short-laced bodice over a white blouse, topped-off with a white cap. Urged on by hunger, I went into the restaurant, sat at a seat overlooking the harbor, and chose the fresh fish chowder and blueberry pie from the menu.

I was so enamored with the chowder, I asked the costumed waitress how it was made. She was a woman in her mid-fifties with an appealing twinkle in her eye, and though the restaurant was filling up, she seemed willing to explain when I asked her for the recipe. She described it in a way so memorable that I didn't need to write anything down and would never forget how to make it. With few words, but mostly expressive gestures, she mimed the ingredients and process.

"First, *beurre,* and two, *oignon,*" she said, and in the air she quickly peeled and chopped an imaginary onion then put a finger to each eye to wipe away supposed tears. The onions went into the pot with the butter in a sweeping s-curved mid-air motion. Then came the *pomme de terre*, the potatoes—maybe 4, maybe more. They were chopped into cubes and just covered with water—very important—just covered. Next, a bit of salt—she sprinkled it in little circles over the invisible pot, then stuck her finger in, shook her head to say it needed a bit more, and added some. Next, she pointed at her watch and said to let them cook till they were just half-done. That was tricky to explain, but I got it. Then, in the air, she cut the fish and gently laid the large pieces on top of the potatoes, added a bit more water to just cover it all and said that when the fish flakes and falls apart—pointing at a smallish piece in my bowl,

"*Voila … Finis*! It's done."

"*C'est magnifique,*" I said, and gave silent applause with upraised hands. She was definitely the most delightful waitress I've ever encountered. I didn't ask for any special explanations about the pie (with ice cream). I just ate it, smiling. And before that, with the chowder, there were rolls—homemade, of course, and as good as my grandmother's were. I smeared them with the local butter that came in a generous mound on a small plate, not in those little plastic packages.

Feeling pleasantly full (and amused), I wandered through the craft shop on the other side of the building to admire the rug hookings that were for sale, then headed to the basement, where there was a small museum that included an old Acadian room with furniture and artifacts. A woman in Acadian dress was demonstrating how to hook a rug on a standing frame made in Cheticamp. She described the process and a bit of rug hooking history as she picked up a narrowly cut strip of wool, and with a wood and metal hook held on the top-side of the stretched burlap on the frame, at the same time, she placed her other hand—the one with the wool strip, underneath, pushed the hook into the burlap and brought a loop of wool to the front.` She continued in this way until she came to the end of a strip and had to reach for another. Her work-in-progress was a small mat with a calm, very blue sea, a red boat and a lighthouse in the distance. It was half-done and it looked like rug hooking was a slow, but relaxing process. Cheticamp is well-known for its hooked rugs, and for a period of time in the 1930's, there was a large cottage industry of women hooking rugs that made their way to be sold in New York City.

I told the woman that my grandmother was from this area.

"What was her name?" she asked.

I replied, "It doesn't sound Acadian. The name was Burns."

"Around here we consider that Acadian. So many men married Acadian women and then became part of the French culture," she told me. "Maybe they weren't pure Acadian by blood, but culturally, they were Acadian." Then she went on to say that one of the best known of the local genealogists was a retired teacher named Edmund Burns.

"You should go up to *Les Trois Pignons* and talk with Edmund—you're probably related," she said.

Baxter gave me a sleepy look when I got into the car to drive the few miles along the water-flanked main street of town. Crab boats were unloading their catches on the wharfs and there was a gentle hum of activity along the sidewalks on both sides of the street. *Les Trois Pignons* (referring to the cultural center/museum's prominent three gables) was easy to spot with its bright red roof. After giving Baxter a quick walk around the parking lot in the rain, I settled him back in the car and went into the building to ask for Edmund Burns. Behind a counter, there were more women in Acadian dress helping tourists visiting the museum portion of the building, and when I asked for the genealogists, they pointed me in the direction of a door to the side.

"Edmund Burns?" I asked as I stepped into the room filled with desks, a computer, book-lined shelves and filing cabinets.

"Yes," he said and got up from his seat to greet me. A tall man, he carried his head slightly to one side, and though quiet and reserved at first, when I told him I was the granddaughter of Nelly Burns, he lit up.

"Nelly from Newton, Massachusetts. She married a Boudrot," I added.

"Yes, yes. I know, sit down," he said, pointing at the chair in front of his desk. "I met her, in Newton, when I was visiting two of my aunts who lived close to her. As a boy it was an exciting adventure to travel from Cheticamp to what we all called the *Boston States* — so I remember everything and everyone from my one visit there. Besides, we're a small family and I've done all the research on us."

He gave me a paper he'd written (in French) about the Burns family and told me that we were second cousins-once-removed. We share a great-grandfather—Michael Burns. Edmund was a gracious man and a great source of Burns information. Sadly, he died in 2009, and I never saw him again. If it were possible to meet with him now, I'd ask him a long list of questions, but at our one meeting, I mostly listened and visited—and added to the Centre's database. He said they were lacking information about all of Nelly's children—my father's generation, and mine. So I filled out their card, listing us all.

Now, a dozen years later, on this trip of looking for all my Acadian grandmothers, my husband came along, and we have a new dog named Louie. He's a wire-haired corgi/terrier mix who looks like a corgi having a bad hair day. On this trip, Louie, like Baxter, years before, had a full romp on Cheticamp Island's beach, where he chased the gulls before turning to his favorite game of digging for small crabs, then jumping back when he'd find one and it started flailing its claws in the direction of his nose. The day was cool enough for him to nap in the car, so we removed as much sand as possible from his dense fur, put him back in the car, and drove to *Les Trois Pignons* for an appointment with Charles Roach, a volunteer at the genealogy center.

He's known as Charlie Dan, his *sobriquet* (nickname), and I liked him from his first greeting. He was shorter and rounder than Edmund—a retired high school math teacher, friendly and happy to help. I told him of my connection to Edmund Burns as he pulled up another chair for my husband. The room looked much the way I remembered from my first visit, except that Charlie Dan had moved into Edmund's old place.

The records at *Les Trois Pignons* are not computerized as they were for the Boudrot search at Isle Madame. Instead, information is kept by paper files, 3x5 index cards, census records, and books. I settled in on the other side of the old wooden desk, told Charlie Dan my grandmother's name, and he set out to find all the Burns generations, following the usual male line.

"I don't want the men—the male line," I told him. "I'm focusing on the women—Nelly's mother, her mother, her mother…"

"You don't want the men?" he said, pushing his coal black hair off his forehead and readjusting his heavy glasses.

"You can tell me who the women married, and everyone's dates, but I mainly want the women," I said.

Charlie Dan leaned forward and warned me that it would take a long time going that route, changing names every time we moved to another generation.

"I know," I agreed. Through experience, he said he thought it might not be possible— given the center's resources, then leaned back in his tilting office chair, folded his hands like extended wings behind his head, and rocked gently back and forth. I waited. My husband and I looked at each other. Charlie Dan looked out the window to the sea, then back at me and the researcher in him responded.

"It won't be easy," he said, "but I might be able to do it"—then got up and started moving from room to room, file to file, shelf to shelf. Sometimes I heard him sigh, or give a jubilant "yes," as he passed my chair. Two hours later, he'd found nine generations of women in my ancestral line—nine of them—all the way back to Jeanne Chebrat.

Jeanne was born in France in 1627, and it's unknown when she sailed across the North Atlantic to settle in *Acadie*. She married Jehan Poitier, who also traveled from France, and together they had two children before Jehan died. Records show that she then married Antoine Gougeon in Port Royal. They had only one child together—the very important Huguette, who was my eighth grandmother. And she had a daughter. Each generation of women had a daughter who had a daughter—all the way to Nelly. And Charlie Dan found them all. Nine generations of foremothers. It was a gift, a heritage of names. I thanked him profusely.

At home, I entered all the names on the computer and on papers in four or five places, so they could never be lost. Then I began researching and adding all the information I could find in a journal the color of the sea.

I learned that I'm not a natural at this

stage of genealogy research, either. It's not just memorizing and keeping generations straight—I'm sloppy and inclined to rush, then have to repeat and rediscover. I needed to call Charlie Dan at *Les Trois Pignons* again. He reassured me that it was o.k. to telephone as often as I needed, and said it was better to call needing short answers rather than long historical ones. I made a note to send another donation to the red-roofed center. Nobody asked for it, but I'm so grateful for their help.

I also made numerous calls to the Acadian scholar, Stephen White, at the *Université de Moncton.* He was equally helpful and patient. I had both genealogists on speed dial and was struggling, but not miserable doing the work. There were times when there were parties and events that came along, and I wanted to stay home with my research, and then, some writing. There were whole days I stayed at the computer in my bathrobe.

I could never get enough information. I was always looking for more—ever grateful that I had their names.

This is What
I Know of Them

Jeanne Chebrat
Huguette Gougeon
Anne Blanchard
Anne Bourgeois
Apolline Arsenault
Marie Magdeleine Bois
Susanne Aucoin
Agathe Ryan
Nelly Burns

My grandmothers
Nine generations of Acadian women
Acadian, because the first of them left France
to settle in a region of eastern Canada,
which they called Acadie
The first of them, one of nearly
80 women considered to be
an ancestral mother
of all Acadians
alive today.

This is their story, and the journey
of how I found them.

Jeanne Chebrat

Born
1626, Loudon, Vienne, Poitou-Charente, France

Died
1688, Port Royal, Acadie

Daughter of
Francoise Chaumoret
b.1607, France
d.1650, France
Antoine Chebrat
b.1600, France
d.1662, France

Spouse
Antoine Gougeon
b.1626, France
d .1678, Port Royal, Acadie
Son of
unknown

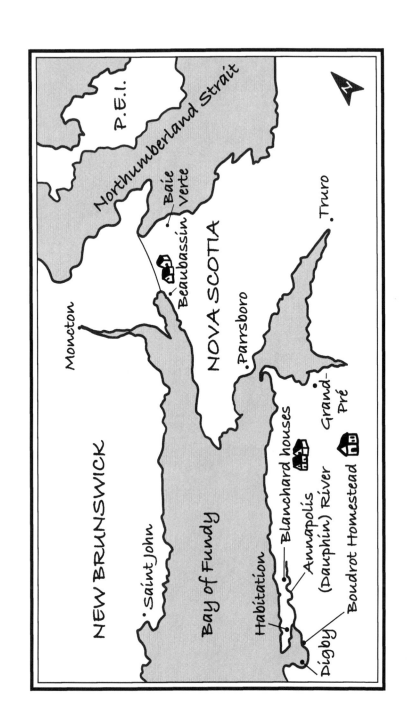

NEW BRUNSWICK

P.E.I.

Northumberland Strait

Baie
verte

Beaubassin

NOVA SCOTIA

Moncton

.Parrsboro

.Truro

Bay of Fundy

.Saint John

Blanchard houses

Grand-
Pré

Annapolis
(Dauphin) River

Habitation

Boudrot Homestead

Digby

Jeanne Chebrat is one of 80 women identified by the Acadian scholar, Stephen White, as a founding mother of all Acadian people alive today. Sixty-eight of these women had daughters, and there is an ongoing mitochondrial project in process regarding their DNA.

Jeanne is the woman in my matrilineal line who traveled the 6- to 8-week ship voyage from France to North America to begin life anew on a sparsely populated continent. She's my ninth grandmother.

There are no records to show when Jeanne arrived in *Acadie*, but it's estimated that she could have made the sailing from France sometime in the mid-1600s. The first time she's found on any North American documents is in the 1671 Port Royal, *Acadie* (now Nova Scotia) census. It's one of the oldest enumerations in all of Canada—written in French, of course. It gives the names and ages of the husband and wife (by her maiden name) and all the children living in a household. Married offspring are counted in the household if they're living with their parents. The 1671 census also includes an

111

occupation for the males, the amount of land each family cultivates, the number of livestock they have, and in some cases, the number of guns they own.

A reference librarian friend of mine who was also researching her family history looked at me with glowing eyes when I showed her the 1671 Acadian census. She stepped back from the computer and said, "Putting together your ancestry with information like this—it's going to be unique, and exciting. This is rich material to work with."

In the era of the first Acadian census, land was measured in *arpents*—an old French unit of length equal to about an acre, and usually divided into long, narrow parcels so that more people could have waterfront property. The census tells us that Jeanne Chebrat and her husband, Antoine Gougon, labourer, which translates to a plowman or farmer, are both age 45 and are cultivating 10 *arpents* of land. In Port Royal, 13 families are listed with 10 or more *arpents*.

The Acadians were living under a feudal-like system with a *signeur*. Under this type of arrangement, royalty grants an expanse of land to an entitled family, they build a large house, and the lands are cultivated by tenants. Those living and working on the land did not own it. In the case of the Acadians, the French crown gave land and rights to a *signeur* who presided over the settlement, but there was usually no grand house, and the *signeur* was rarely present. In these feudal-type settlements, farmers, especially those with sons and other strong-bodied relatives capable of hard labor, cultivated large areas of land. Skilled craftsmen, on the other hand, needed few *arpents*.

In 1671, Jeanne Chebrat and Antoine Gougon had 20 cattle and 17 sheep. But most important for me, they had their only child—14-year-old Huguette, my eighth grandmother. When I saw Huguette's name, I felt a tremendous wave of gratitude that she, their only child, was born. I was struck by how random and magical our existence is. If there had been no Huguette, there would be no me, or any of the many other lives that came from her, and will continue through my line.

Michel Boudrot and Michelle Aucoin, ninth grandparents on my grandfather's side of the family, are also on the 1671 census—and there are other families who intermarried with mine. Michel Boudrot is 71, a farmer, and his wife, Michelle Aucoin, is 53. Those living in the household include three married children: Francois 29 (in my direct line); Jeanne 25; Marguerite 20; and unmarried: Charles 22; Marie 18; Jehan 16; Habraham 14; Michel 12; Olivier 10; Claude 8; and Francois 5. Considering Michel and Michelle's age, the young offspring listed must belong to their married children. The household had 20 cattle, 12 sheep, and 8 *arpents* of land.

At the bottom of the last page of the census, the enumerator, Laurent Molins, identified himself as a *Religioux Cordelier*—a Franciscan missionary. The men of this order were called *cordelier* because of the cords they wore around their waists. Laurent Molins added some notes to his pages, writing that Pierre Melancon, tailor, refused to answer, then in parenthesis wrote that Pierre has a wife and seven children. The *Cordelier's* next entry is that Pierre Melanson, tailor, "would not give his age nor the number of animals, but his wife's answers concerning their possessions was just as crazy." Continuing his notes, "Estienne Robichaud, farmer, did not want to see the census taker and left, telling his wife not to tell about the livestock or land." And my favorite — a note about Pierre Lanoue, a cooper. "When asked his age, he said he felt fine but would not give an answer!"

The final tally for Port Royal in 1671, with a few possible hold-outs missing, was 392 people, 482 cattle and 524 sheep. No total is given for guns.

Looking back at the original passenger list from the *Saint Jehan*, the only ship's passenger list documenting travel from France to *Acadie* during this era that's ever been found, it's interesting to note again that 35 years after the *Saint Jehan* left

France in 1636, most of the people who came on that sailing were no longer in Port Royal at the time of the first Acadian census.

The *Saint Jehan* passengers were not the first Europeans to settle in *Acadie*. In the 1630s, small contingencies of people came, and some of them were a part of Samuel de Champlain's expeditions. Champlain, sometimes called the *Father of New France*, began exploring North America in 1603. Among his many skills, he was a cartographer and navigator. He and his men established a colony in 1604, at Saint Croix Island on the border of present day New Brunswick and Maine. When choosing the location, they thought the island would provide safe anchorage and be defendable. In the summer, it looked ideal, but the first winter was bitter. When the Saint Croix River froze, the men felt vulnerable to attack, although there were no intrusions ever reported. The very real and devastating event for them was an outbreak of Scurvy. It killed 35 of the men—nearly half of them. Those who survived abandoned the site and sailed back to France the following summer.

Estimations are that between the years 1600 and 1800, almost a million men around the western world died of Scurvy. The deaths on Saint Croix, from one of the oldest-known nutritional disorders, came before the discovery that the disease is caused by a Vitamin C deficiency. The human body doesn't produce its own ascorbic acid, so Vitamin C must be obtain from food—especially fresh fruits and vegetables. A poor diet during the winter spent on Saint Croix Island was the probable cause of the death of so many of the men.

Those on the island were also inadequately prepared for the severity of the winter. Champlain wrote in his journal:

It was difficult to know this country without having wintered there: for on arriving in summer everything is very pleasant on account of the woods, the beautiful landscapes and the fine fishing for the many kinds of fish we found there. There are six months of winter in that country.

The summer after so many died on Saint Croix, French merchant, explorer, and nobleman Pierre Dugua de Mons, Samuel de Champlain, and others returned to North America. They explored as far south as Cape Cod, then sailed across the *Baie Francaise* (Bay of Fundy) looking for a sheltered location. Their goal was to find an area with a reliable source of water, plenty of farmland to grow food, plus access to timber for building materials and heating. They chose land beside the *Rivière Dauphin*.

In the summer of 1605, the men built a French-style *Habitation*, which was fort-like, with buildings for housing, supplies, and workshops around a central courtyard. Today, there is a replica on the approximate site of the original *Habitation*, along the *Rivière Dauphin*, renamed the Annapolis River by the British. They also changed Port Royal's name to Annapolis Royal. For the builders of the original *Habitation* in Champlain's era, the devastation of the previous year's outbreak of Scurvy on Saint Croix Island taught them the importance of a good diet. They also learned the value of social interactions and occasions during the long and often severe winters. And importantly, the native Mi'kmaq taught them how to feast from the bounty of fish and game in this new land.

Champlain established *L' Ordre de Bon Temps* (the Order of Good Cheer) to ensure good health and morale over the winter at the *Habitation*. During the first years there, journal entries were made, telling how the members took turns fishing and hunting for the best fish and fowl they could find. These were a feature of the nightly banquets they held. In the evenings, the men gathered in a large hall that was also used for their Neptune Theatre performances. For the celebratory feasts, the men marched into the dining room, with guests following, each with a platter of food (hopefully some with vegetables and fruit) in hand. It's recorded that these feasts were attended by the Mi'kmaq of all ages and genders. Sometimes 20 or 30 of them were present, and the chiefs of the Indian nations were treated as guests and equals.

Somewhere, in an unknown drawer, I have a certificate declaring I'm a member of *L'Ordre de Bon Temps* — it's a document bought by my parents in a tourist shop long ago.

On a regular diet of fresh food from the sea and land, and their own wine and bread, only four men died of Scurvy during Champlain and company's first year in Port Royal. But it all came to an end as a permanent settlement when the King of France revoked Pierre Dugua de Mons' fur trading monopoly, and in the fall of 1607, the men abandoned the *Habitation*. Most sailed back to France, leaving the buildings to the care of the Mi'kmaq, with chief Membertou in charge. Champlain sailed in the opposite direction—up the Saint Lawrence River, founding Quebec City in 1608.

Those arriving on the *Saint Jehan* in 1636 settled with a group of French who had come earlier, near the LaHave River, but later moved on to the *Rivière Dauphin*, where Champlain's *Habitation* had been and where the land was better for cultivation. There, the North Mountain shields the river's valley from the winds and fog of the Bay of Fundy, and the South Mountain forms the other side of the valley. Today this area contains one-third of all the farmland in Nova Scotia and grows a wider range of crops than anywhere else in the Maritimes. An added bonus to being on the *Rivière Dauphin*, near the *Habitation*, was that Champlain and his men had established such good relations with the native Mi'kmaq that the newcomers could reap the benefits of their friendship.

I spent all the summers of my childhood in Nova Scotia, and now my husband and I live here six months of the year. There's so much to love about this peninsula province, but one of my favorite things is that each of its shores is uniquely different.

We're on the Northumberland Strait side, across from Prince Edward Island. Soft winds blow most of the time, and our grounds are flowing in wildflowers and weeds—whatever the wind brings in. The most common trees are furs and spruce, birch, and the deciduous hackmatack. Waist-high valerian, joe pye weed, and symphytum wave their showy heads across the property to the cat tails and fern in the driveway's ditch. Deep orange tiger lilies and

giant daisies replace the earlier-blooming blue-
flag iris and lupine. Wild roses and indian
plums grow in concentrated patches. The air
is fresh, and the wind makes everything—me
included, feel so alive.

I once naively tried to keep a minimalist
Japanese garden in the middle of our circular
drive, until we finally surrendered to the
intentions of nature. Each spring, we greet what
reappears from last year, and then are surprised
by what has blown in to our space and takes root
in the current year. Lost under all that botanical
self-expression are large rocks we long ago placed
in Zen-style, that are now plant-covered and
nowhere to be seen. Our Australian Shephards
are buried under the sheltering hackmatack
tree at one end of the stone-lined circle and a
graceful birch stands at the other. In between is
colorful and uncultivated chaos. A friend from
England visiting Nova Scotia for the first time,
said, "Things we struggle so hard to cultivate in
England just grow in the ditches here."

On the Northumberland Strait shore, the
soil and the beaches are a ferric oxide, rusty
color, and the waters are warmer than anywhere
north of the Carolinas. The sandbars go out

for long distances, get heated by the sun, and warm the water. I know I sound like a tourist bureau—but it's all true.

The Annapolis Valley has a very different appearance. It's farmland, and the Bay of Fundy is more powerful looking than the Northumberland Strait.

I had been to the Valley, but never with Acadians in mind. Now that I know about ancestors who settled along the river, I'm anxious to return—this time with an historical agenda and a sense of adventure.

Once we planned our trip to Port Royal, my husband and I decided to go by water—traveling *on* the Bay of Fundy, rather than driving around its shores. We know the shoreline of Fundy very well. We even named one of our dogs Fundy, but we haven't spent much time on the waters of the Bay. I wanted to go to Port Royal to soak up the area and imagine what the landscape might have looked like when my ancestors arrived. Since so much of the early Acadians' transportation involved the seas, bays, and rivers of Nova Scotia, it seemed the appropriate way to arrive, even though we'd have a car on a lower deck and all the conveniences of a modern ferry at hand.

It's about a two-hour drive from our home to the Bay Ferry Terminal in Saint John, New Brunswick, then two-and-a-half hours to cross to Digby on the ship, *The Rose Fortune*. The ferry travels at 21-22 knots an hour and on the day of our travel, the Bay was calm.

"It's not always like this," one of the stewards told us. "It can be rough out here in the winter. Oh, nothing like what the Newfoundland crossings can bring. They're something else. Fundy never freezes, so we don't have icebergs to steer around like the Newfoundland fleet has. But we've got short, tricky swells to deal with."

I asked him what the water temperature that day was. Three to 6 degrees Celsius (37.4 - 42.8 degrees Fahrenheit), he told me. A fellow passenger asked how powerful the engine is (20,000 horsepower). The *Rose Fortune* gets little rest. It travels from Saint John to Digby, Nova Scotia every day except Christmas and New Year's.

"We have to put extra runs on during lobster season—she's loaded down with tractor trailers then," our steward added, then he had to leave when the ferry's intercom called him back to his duties.

My husband and I headed for the snack bar, then brought our food out to the aft deck to enjoy the sun. Sitting back from the rail and looking out to the water with no land in sight, we were suddenly astonished by the sight of an enormous whale breaching the waves. We quickly rushed to a spot by the outside rail and watched the whale hurl its massive tonnage high in the air as it arched out of the water, making amazing turns and gaining impressive heights. The spectacular display happened three or four times, to the enormous roar of the passengers on both the upper and lower aft decks. The whale looked like it was playing to the crowd, responding to the roars, until it went crashing downward and disappeared underwater. Though we stood glued to our spot and waited, it didn't return. The aft-deck eaters just looked at each other—stunned into silence, then broke into excited applause. The deckhand standing beside me was as thrilled as any of us. She said it was the first whale she'd seen on any of the crossings this season.

I rushed back to the table where our food and belongings were to find the whale brochure I'd picked up when we got onboard, searching through it for a whale image that matched the markings we'd just seen on *our* whale. There were five or six pictured, and I found an image whose markings were the same as the one we'd seen. It was the Right Whale, making it an even more amazing sighting, since it's on the endangered species list.

Whalers gave the Right Whale its name because they thought it was the correct whale to hunt. They're docile, swim close to shore, and their blubber is filled with oil, which the fishermen coveted. Today, North Atlantic Right Whales are threatened by habitat loss, humans, entanglement in fishing gear, and collisions with ships. On that day, we marveled at the sight of the whale, hoping that it would live a long and productive life for the future of the species. And also wishing that in the future, others of its kin would be in the mighty Bay of Fundy to astonish other ferry-goers.

As we all settled down and bonded with our fellow whale watchers on the aft deck, the ferry continued on its way, then quietly pulled into the dock at Digby Neck.

We had come to the *Rivière Daulphin* valley, now the Annapolis River, ready to look, but also to locate the home sites of my Port Royal ancestors along both sides of this beautiful, meandering river. Weeks earlier, while visiting with Stephen White, the genealogist at the *Université de Moncton*, he showed me a reproduction of a 1707 map of the river, including Port Royal as well as *Belleisle*, which is on the north side of the river and closer to Bridgetown. The map/plan was in the Canadian Historical Atlas and follows the water's meanderings from the Bay of Fundy to Bridgetown. It also shows the locations and names of the Acadian-built marshes, but most excitedly for me, it identifies and names all of the 1707 family home sites along the river.

Scanning the family names marked on both sides of the river is a revisit of old census lists and the names I heard on Nelly's porch—*Robichaud, Melanson, Bourg, Doucet, Dugas, Brun, LeBlanc, Hebert, Boudrot, Blanchard,* and so many more.

On my reproduction of the plan, I first searched along the south side of the river and found Francois Boudrot's home site. Michel Boudrot and Michelle Aucoin, found on the 1671 census, are not listed. Michel, who rose to the rank of Lieutenant Governor (Magistrate) died between 1688 and 1693, making him 88 to 93 years old at the time of death. Michelle Aucoin died in 1706, at age 87. Their son Francois was probably living on the original family land. He is their first child and is in my direct paternal line.

While researching the earliest locations of the Acadians, I came across documentation of the building projects that had been completed. Of interest was a letter written on October 15,

1687. In it, Michel Boudrot, who was Advisor and Lieutenant in *Acadie*, describes some of the work that was completed at that time. The letter reads:

"We, Michel Boudrot, Lieutenant-General in Acadie, with the older settlers of the land, certify that the deceased mister d'Aunay Charnisay, formerly the King's Governor of the coast of Acadie, constructed three forts along this coast; the first one at Pentagouêt, the second at the Saint-Jean River (in 1645 only), and the third at Port-Royal; these forts were well supplied with all the canons and munitions required! There are three hundred regular men to defend these forts.

We certify also that the late d'Aulnay Charnisay ordered the construction of two mills; one was powered by water, the other by wind power and he ordered that they build at Port-Royal five pinasses, several dories, and two small ships of seventy tons each. As well as two farms or manors and associated buildings; houses as well as barns and stables (...)

We certify that the above is true as we have seen this; we have signed this in good faith at Port-Royal on October 15, 1687, in the presence of Mr.

de Menneval, King's Governor of all of Acadie, and Mr. Petit, Grand Vicar for the Grand Bishop of Québec, and the vicar of this place Port-Royal.

Also having signed;
Mr. Boudrot, Lieutenant-Governor;
François Gaunizzot (Gautherot) Bourgeois;
Pierre Martin; Mathieu Martin; ClaudeTériot;
d'Entremont, King's prosecutor.
Also marked by: Antoine Bourg,
Pierre Bouet (Doucet), Denis (Daniel) LeBlanc,
Abraham Dugast.

On our present trip, there are no old Acadian mills, or houses, or barns to seek out and visit. I only have family names on the 1707 plan to show where ancestors once lived. And I'm grateful to have that.

There is no Jeanne Chebrat and Antoine Gougeon home site shown. Jeanne Chebrat died in 1688, and her husband, Antoine Gougeon died in 1678. They are both buried in Port Royal.

But I have followed their only child, Huguette, on all the census lists, and know that she married Guillame Blanchard—and there are two Blanchard homesteads clearly identified on the map.

Huguette Agathe Gougeon

Born
about 1657, Port Royal, Acadie

Died
1717, Port Royal, Acadie

Daughter of
Jeanne Chebrat
b. 1627, France
d. 1688, Port Royal, Acadie
Antoine Gougeon
b. 1626, France,
d. 1678, Port Royal

Spouse
Guillaume Blanchard
b. 1650, Port Royal, Acadie
d. 1716, Port Royal, Acadie

Son of
Jeanne Radegonde Lambert
b. 1621, France
d. Unknown
Jean Blanchard
b. 1611, France
d. Unknown

On our first morning in Digby, we woke to an ethereal fog. From the window of the hotel, the town appeared to be floating over water, until it slowly turned into something real instead of imaginary. By the time breakfast was over, the sun had claimed its dominance, and it looked like it would be a glorious day.

We left the hotel in high spirits, setting out to explore the river, the marshes, and home sites where my ancestors had originally settled. In the car, we had a copy of the 1707 historical plan showing the locations of families who had lived along the *Rivière Dauphin* (Annapolis River) at that time. We were also carrying a Nova Scotia Atlas, a Nova Scotia tourist map, and two 26 x 38 inch topographical maps of the area in 1:50,000 dimension. We were definitely over-prepared, but wanted to have every reference material we might possibly need.

Before leaving home, we had studied the maps, checking and then comparing relation-ships of home sites to the meanderings of the river. We named the pronounced river turnings *short omegas, mid-sized ones, and tall omegas* —because they looked like the Greek letter omega. This helped us to plot where we would be in relation to the river as we drove along side it—and to find where the home sites we were interested in were located. That the river moved in its own graceful way, and gave us images we could use in orienting ourselves, was a gift. In preparation mode, and without trying very hard, we had mental images of the river and the names of marshes memorized.

Sadly, all of the Acadian houses of the area were burned by the British around 1755, at the time of the Expulsion. Homes were reduced to foundations filled with ash and objects, or fragments of them that could survive a fire. Most of the foundations are now buried under dirt and foliage and are no longer visible. Still, we wanted to get a feeling for the place and know where houses once stood. The whole thing had the sense of a historical treasure hunt, and we had all our maps!

The Francois Boudrot and Marie-Madeleine Belleveau location was the closest to our starting point, so we began there. The land wasn't easy to find by sight because the Boudrots settled on the estuary section of the river where there were none of our *omega* shapes to use—no river meanderings to observe on this wide and straight section of the *Rivière Dauphin.* We thought about measuring distances and comparing the 1707 map to the modern ones, but we had no way of knowing how the roads had changed in 310 years. On the map, the Boudrot home site appeared to be close to a creek, but we couldn't find any obvious creek, and drove up and down one section of the road three times with no luck.

On the fourth trip, I noticed a sign for a dog kennel at the bottom of a long uphill driveway, and we turned in and drove to the top. Since the kennel was a public business, it didn't feel invasive to pull up into their property. The stunning view at the top of the drive gave us a broad and unencumbered look at the river. We could see marshes and dykes along this south side of the *Dauphin* and across to the dykes and marshes on its north side.

We'd arrived at a large working farm, and off in one of the fields, a man on a tractor was moving bales of hay into a barn. Ahead of our stopping point at the end of the long driveway, a van was pulled up to the dog kennel door and two people were unloading a Golden Retriever with all its paraphernalia. We didn't want to interfere with the dog's drop off, so we walked over to the edge of a woodpile to take in the glorious view of the river and beyond. Both my husband and I pulled out our phones to take photos and didn't notice the man from the tractor approach until we heard him ask, "Are you folks lost, or did you just stop to take some pictures?"

"It's beautiful here," I said. "But we did stop for a purpose. We've been driving up and down the road for the last half hour, looking for the Boudrot land on this map, and can't find it. We thought maybe you could help us."

"I've had Boudrots searching around this location before," he said. "You're close, and I can definitely help."

He told us he grew up on this farm, and when he and his brothers played, there was an old Acadian stone foundation with lots of ash in it further up the hill. As kids, they found old nails and things there, but said the foundation is overgrown now.

"You can't even get to it. It was the Dugas place, before they were burned out during the Expulsion." Pointing to the east of where we stood, he told us, "There, just beyond the grove of trees, is where the Boudrots would have been. You almost found it."

Then he turned towards the river and, drawing a long line with his broad hand, he followed the water below and said, "There's the marsh they cultivated and the dykes they built. The Dugas and Boudrots — and a few more. Together, the families would have created the dykes and continue to maintain them during their lifetimes. The Acadians came from the part of France where they knew how to dike the waterways, and they brought that knowledge here with them."

Our host, John Brown, retired Royal Canadian Mounted Police, continued, "Because the systems they created are so important to the environmental health of this river area, the government today is maintaining them and mowing the marshes. It's fragile, so it's mown with appropriate-sized equipment, then I go down with my large tractor to collect the hay the government people move close to the road for farmers to pick up to feed their cattle. I was just moving some of it to the barn when you arrived," he said. Clearly we'd picked the perfect place to stop and ask questions.

We talked long after the car dropping off the Golden Retriever drove off, learning interesting places where we should stop along the river. John also went into the house and got another map he had, and showed it to us, pointing out the LeBlanc settlement and telling us that if we had any LeBlancs in our family tree, we should stop at a house there.

"The man who lives there knows everything about them," he told us. The LeBlancs are the largest of all the Acadian families, and since I have one direct link to the LeBlancs, we later stopped by the house, but there was no one home.

Leaving John, with an invitation to come back anytime, we drove a short way east and found a small lay-by to pull off, get out of the car, and linger on the Boudrot land. Down on a level with the expansive marsh across the road, we marveled again at the beauty of the peaceful river, and the engineering skills the Acadians needed to transform the salt marshes at the tidal river's edge into fertile soil to grow their hay, grain, and flax. Quickly, I saw the little creek we'd been unable to find when we drove past three times. It added a calming effect to the scene, and I soaked up the Boudrot presence—naturally thinking of my father who had a strong spiritual esthetic and would have loved it here.

The Boudrot *arpents* probably reached far up the hill, behind the unoccupied house that stood near the road, but the land was steep and overgrown with shrubs and we decided not to go up there. Because we'd experienced the river and marshes from the Dugas property when we visited with John Brown, we knew that the Boudrots—Michelle and Michel, Francois and Marie Magdeleine, and their children—would have had a similar vantage point, living and being nourished by the same soul-enriching view.

Leaving the Boudrot land, we drove into the lovely and very British-looking town of

Annapolis Royal, then crossed the river, and headed west. The large Dugas/Brown farm, high on the hill, and the Boudrot land were easy to locate from across the river as we drove to the replica of Champlain's *Habitation*. At the *Habitation* kiosk, we found we could purchase copies of the same 1707 plan we were using, and I wondered if this was where my parents had bought the certificate of membership in *L'Ordre de Bon Temps*, the one they'd given me so many years ago. Sadly, my father, if he had been here, didn't know how close he was to the original Boudrot ancestral land.

Though the day was warm and sunny, the rooms inside the old fort felt dark and damp. It was much more pleasant to be outside, under the trees by the river. After a refreshing walk, we spoke with a guide who told us about the Melanson Settlement, just down the road. Since John Brown had also recommended a visit there, we headed back to it.

The stop was productive. Walking the pathways leading in the direction of the river, and reading the informative signage about Acadian life up and down both sides of the *Dauphin*, gave us a solid orientation to how the people in the area lived. There's a valuable teaching element in the row of mounted plaques describing and illustrating where foundations had been found and what the buildings of the former village might have looked like. The signs showed copies of census records in original script of all the early families who lived along the river—and how they grouped themselves together in what were called family villages. Somewhere in my reading, an author called these groupings "clanhoods." I give my apologies to whoever coined the clever description, but I'm unable to find the source again in order to give the author proper credit. These "clanhoods" were small groups of relatives, including those who married into the family, who lived and worked together for the profit of all. Together, they built and maintained the dykes to give them marshland to cultivate, and shared in many other endeavors, no doubt.

The British of the era were puzzled by the Acadians because they converted the salt marshes into land that could be cultivated instead of chopping down trees and clearing the forests in order to have land to farm. From an original source, writings from the Sieur de Dièreville, who came to Port Royal from Normandy in 1699, and who many consider to be the most important reporter of life along the Dauphin. Dièreville wrote:

It costs a great deal to prepare the lands which they wish to cultivate. To grow wheat, the marshes which are inundated by the Sea at high tide, must be drained; these are called Lowlands, and they are quite good, but what labour is needed to make them for cultivations! The ebb and flow of the Sea cannot easily be stopped, but the Acadians succeed in doing so by means of great dykes, called aboiteaux.

Dièreville was almost right. The aboiteaux, with their clappers, let fresh water run off the marsh, and kept the sea water out—they are a part of the dyke, not a name for a dyke.

In paintings of haying season on the marsh, women are shown raking in the fields along with the men. Although I haven't found much written about the roles of Acadian women, I have read that they shared in the workings of a farm—much like farm women have been doing for centuries. They carried out the domestic chores, took care of the cooking, the children, and the chickens. Some say they were responsible for the care of the fruit trees, especially the apple orchards, which were important to the Acadians. In the 1698 Port Royal census, in addition to counting the amount of people, livestock, guns and land, they also counted the number of fruit trees. In that year, there were 575 adults and children, 982 cattle, 1136 sheep, 568 hogs, 1275 arpents of cultivated land, 82 guns, 8 servants, and 1584 fruit trees.

The magazine, *Saltscapes,* in an article about apples says:

Fortunately, the early Acadian settlers were drinking men, bringing their hard apple cider tradition with them when they came to settle around Annapolis Royal in the early 1600s. Champlain's 1605 diary notes "the cold was so intense that the cider was divided by an axe and measured out by the pound." This is the first recorded use of an apple product in North America. Apples were not native here, but the Acadians quickly established orchards at their new settlements, planting seeds and small trees brought over from France. Cider production was thoroughly transplanted to the New World.

I like to think that the women, besides preserving and cooking apples, also got to enjoy their own glass of cider. The *Saltscape* article goes on to say that by the time of the Deportation, there were 18,000 Acadians and they had spread an equal number of apple trees across the Annapolis Valley alone.

The women also produced most of the clothing for the family—by spinning, weaving, and knitting—using the flax grown on the reclaimed salt marshes and wool from the sheep in the fields. There are tailors mentioned in the early census records, but I think it's fair to credit the women with weaving any fabric that was not imported.

Work done by females, no doubt, had a communal component to it. Women, by nature, do a lot of chores together. At times, when I've been involved in fibre arts, I usually did much of it with others—spinning wool in a group, hoisting my spinning wheel into the trunk of the car to drive to a place where a group of women would spin in community and knit with one another. I grew up with my grandmother, Nelly, knitting for her family on her front porch with neighborhood women, carrying on the tradition of her female ancestors.

Knowing the rate of fertility and excellent infant survival of the Acadians, living among family members and multiple generations must have been of enormous help to the mothers of these large families. Huguette, according to the records I have found, had nine children. Some secondary sources say that she had 12. Her first child was born when she was about 17, and if she had 12 children, the last one would have been born when she was 42.

In what has been written about the general history of the fertility of the Acadian women, most of the reporting gives credit to good food and a healthy lifestyle for the well-being of the mother, as well as the low infant mortality rates. But females supporting the other women in their families and villages surely played an important role. There must have been strong cooperation among the women in these *clanhood* clusters for their way of life to prosper. We'll never know who all the midwives were—or the women healers. But we do know that they were essential to the health of their people. Their efforts, and the benefits of a communal-type life for Acadian women raising large families, must have played essential roles.

On our visit, we walked around the Melanson Settlement twice because the information was so intriguing. We were then ready to head east to *Belleisle Marsh*, and reached for the atlas and maps, and set the car's GPS so that we could see the river's meanderings as we drove alongside.

There are two Blanchard homesteads noted on the 1707 plan, and census records showed Huguette had married Guillaume Blanchard. The first time I saw her on a document was in the 1671 Port Royal census, when at 14, she was the only child living with her mother and father (Jeanne Chebrat and Antoine Gougeon). In the 1678 census, Huguette is listed with her husband, Guillaume Blanchard, and three children—a girl, age 5, and two boys, ages 3 and 6 months. The family was living with

Guillaume's parents, Jean Blanchard and Radegonde Lambert, in *Belleisle*.

In the Port Royal census of 1700, Huguette and Guillaume had eight children living at home (Marie, the eldest, was married and living away). The boys were listed first, in their birth order: Rene, 23; Antoine, 21; Jean, 13; and Guillaume, 10. The four girls were: Jeanne, 18; Anne, 16; Elisabeth, 11; and Madelaine, 8. The family also reported cultivating 30 *arpents* and owning 26 cattle, 39 sheep, and 3 guns.

Guillaume's parents were not listed on the census of 1700, and were probably deceased. (In the census of 1686, Jeanne Radegonde Lambert, his mother, was 65, and father, Jean, was 75.) Guillaume's brother, Martin Blanchard, was also in this census. He was 55, married to Marguerite Guillebaud, age 31. They had four children: Rene, 23; Pierre, 8; Marie, 25; Marguerite, 11, as well as 24 cattle, 10 sheep, 10 arpents and 1 gun. It's interesting to note that on this 1700 census, Hugette was listed by her middle name, Agathe.

The Blanchard home sites seemed easy to find, thanks to our study of the 1707 plan, the current maps we'd gathered, the car's GPS, and the visibility of the meandering river. By using and comparing them all, we found the Blanchard land and in a sense, we found them.

It could have been enough to know where their land was, but I was still curious about the *Belleisle* marsh, and at home, when I went online, I found references to archeology digs that took place there. One website lead me to a university master's degree thesis in archeology. After reading it, I now know more than I could have ever imagined knowing about pottery shards, glass fragments, pottery sources in the 1600s, styles of buildings of that century, and even materials used to seal cracks in the walls of structures—the kinds of findings archeologists are looking for and finding in their excavations.

In 1983, researchers from the Nova Scotia Museum and *Université Sainte-Anne* unearthed pre-expulsion foundations during a dig at the village of *Belleisle*. One was an Acadian house built around 1680. It was large, with amenities—a spacious baking oven inside the house, an herb garden, and a number of other conveniences. Dr. Marc Lavoie wrote in his master's thesis, the one I found online, that "this dig helped to shatter the textbook idea that the Acadians were peasants living in misery." As David Christianson of the Nova Scotia Museum explained, "The settlers' home would have been part of a highly developed environment that included a kitchen garden, animal pens, a dovecote and so on."

The archaeologists discovered that what they thought was one site, was two houses — one built on top of an earlier one. "Both houses exhibited evidence of having been destroyed by burning, presumably at the time of the Expulsion. *House One* had also been damaged by fire at an undetermined earlier date before being rebuilt." An unusual feature of some Acadian kitchens (including this one) was that the bake oven was accessible from indoors. In France, the winter weather wasn't cold enough to affect the bread-baking process, but in Canada, indoor access to the oven was essential.

In Dr. Lavoie's dating of the ceramic fragments and the pieces of clay tobacco pipes, (it's said that both women and men smoked pipes) found in the *Belleisle* houses suggest that they were occupied during the first half of the eighteenth century.

After being at *Belleisle* and walking the marshes, I was intrigued by what the archeologists found, but taunted by the idea of *House One* and *House Two*. Does anybody know who lived in these houses? Do archeologists care about identifying people with places? I also had some unanswered questions about those fragments of pottery and glass, but back to *House One* and *House Two*. I reminded myself that I'm not an archeologist, but I wanted to know—could Huguette have lived in one of these houses?

Without doing any thinking or preparing in advance, I phoned *Université Sainte-Anne*, the last known location I could find for Marc Lavoie, the man whose Master's thesis I read online, to speak to him in person. *Saint Anne's* is a francophone university in Church Point, Nova Scotia, about an hour away from *Belleisle*. The *Université Sainte-Anne* and the *Université de Moncton* in New Brunswick are the only French language universities in the Maritime Provinces.

When the phone was answered in French (of course) I quickly said to the woman who answered that my high school French wasn't up to her speed, and she laughed (the universal language), and we went on in English. There was a Marc Lavoie on the faculty, she said, and on the first try of ringing through to him, he didn't answer his phone and I didn't leave a message. An hour later, I phoned again, this time asking the receptionist for his extension number so that I wouldn't have to keep bothering her. She said it was no bother at all, gave me his extension number, then told me that he was probably in his office by now. She just saw him leaving the mail room and heading in that direction.

The woman rang me through, and Marc Lavoie answered his phone. He was receptive, informative, and treated all of my questions seriously. Based on the first question I asked, (I thought I'd start out with glass shards), he cleared up some mysteries about glass and pottery fragments and then went on to explain about his theory that the Acadians had a stratified society. To begin with, not all Acadian houses are the same size, he told me. *House One* on *Belleisle*, the larger of the two he worked on, had fine sets of pottery and lots of it. Other findings on the site brought him to the conclusion that the occupants were living at a high economic level, and that the owner was perhaps a merchant. He said that the pottery fragments found there matched the level of some of those found in the upper economic level of homes of the same era found in New England.

We had some more conversation about what was found at his *Belleisle* dig, and I came to the end of my ability to ask any more questions— except for the one I most wanted to ask. A voice inside reminded me that there were 70 homesteads along the river with 49 family names. Ten homes with nine different family names were in *Belleisle*. On the 1707 map, the Blanchards have two houses listed side by side. Could it possibly be that one of the houses Marc Lavoie excavated was Huguette's? What were the odds?

"Do you know whose homes *House One* and *House Two* were?" I asked.

"Yes," he said. "They're both Blanchard houses."

Unbelievable, wonderful, Hugette!

I heard myself silently exclaim. "That's the family I'm researching," I said out loud to Marc, and added a resounding "Perfect."

The thing is, when you get knee-deep in research like this, the rest of the world fades away and these pieces of information take on enormous significance. I mentally waltzed around this gem of news, and then Marc Lavoie told me that he would be taking his students to the Blanchard houses very soon, and if I gave him my phone number, he'd call, and I could meet him and his students on site to learn and explore with them.

"Be sure and bring your rubber boots," he said. "The marsh is soft. That's why the foundations are so well preserved. And don't try to go there alone. The last person who did had an accident."

I thanked him and hung up the phone. My husband was in his office working on some deep scientific problem when I went bursting in to tell him the news. Luckily, he'd been on the trip to Port Royal and *Belleisle* searching for my foremothers with me. For a long time, he'd been hearing about adventures in finding them, or been along with me on the trips to their locations, and with the news that the Blanchards owned *House One* and *House Two*, he joined me in celebration and asked to definitely go along on any future *Belleisle* archeological digs.

Huguette's husband, Guillaume Blanchard, and several of their children have some notoriety. The *Canadian Biographical* site credits Guillaume, his two sons, and Pierre Tibaudeau, who the 1707 plan of Port Royal shows living across the river from the Blanchards, with sailing the Blanchard's boat to Chepody (Shepody) River in present-day New Brunswick, exploring it over several years, and in 1699, establishing a settlement there known as *Village des Blanchard*. This village was in what is now Hillsboro, and other websites note that today there are many Blanchards in the area. Some of Guillaume and Huguette's older children are reported to have stayed in *Village des Blanchard*. My guess is that Huguette and the younger children stayed where they were in either *House One* or *House Two* in *Belleisle* while all of this was going on.

Leaving the research or speculation to the scholars, I returned to what I know of them. Huguette's fifth child and third daughter, Anne Blanchard, is my seventh grandmother. The 1707 map that directed our Port Royal searches shows that the Bourgeois family lived just up the river from the Blanchard family. Marie, Huguette's oldest daughter, age eighteen in 1700, married Charles Bourgeois, and the couple went to live in *Beaubasin*, a new settlement founded by Jacque Bourgeois, the grandfather of her husband, Charles.

Anne, my seventh grandmother, was 16 and living at home in 1700, but I know from researching later census records that she will marry Claude Bourgeois, the brother of Charles, and they will also move to *Beaubassin*.

Two sisters marrying two brothers and moving to *Beaubassin* — a place I know well. I now go to this beautiful marsh, just 30 minutes from my home, with a new awareness and sense of connection. It's not just a marshland I've painted and loved. I have ancestors who lived there!

Anne Blanchard

Born
1682, Port Royal, Acadie

Died
unknown

Daughter of
Huguette Gougeon
b.1657, Port Royal, Acadie
d.1717, Port Royal. Acadie
Guillaume Blanchard
b.1650, Port Royal, Acadie
d. unknown

Spouse
Claude Bourgeois
b.1674, Port Royal, Acadie
d. unknown
Son of
Anne Dugas
b.1668, France
d. unknown
Charles Bourgeois
b.1646
d. unknown

Anne Blanchard, my seventh grandmother, was born in the middle of Huguette's brood of 10 or more children. If the records are correct, Anne proved to be a strong woman—surviving through the deportation years, and according to some sources, living to be 88 years old.

She married Claude Bourgeois and left Port Royal, joining her sister and husband in *Beaubassin*. The village of *Beaubassin* is on the isthmus of *Chignecto*, separating the Bay of Fundy from the Northumberland Strait, and is the little neck of land that keeps today's Nova Scotia from being an island. The area grew to be one of the largest and most prosperous settlements in *Acadie* while the two sisters, Anne and Marie Blanchard were living there.

Chignecto runs 10 miles long and 17 miles wide at its narrowest point, and there's a portage route along a part of the Misoguash River that the Mi'kmaq used to travel between the Cumberland Basin on the Bay of Fundy side and Baie Verte on the Northumberland Strait.

Jacques Bourgeois, grandfather to the

husbands of the Blanchard sisters, explored the area of the Isthmus along with other men from Port Royal. They obviously thought the large *Tintemarre Marsh* showed enormous potential for diking Fundy's waters, and creating rich land to farm. When he lived in Port Royal, Bourgeois traded with New Englanders and taught himself English. He no doubt saw the *Chignecto* location as strategic for trading with other parts of New France, New England, and the area they called Canada—today's Quebec. Bourgeois is cited as a surgeon, farmer, and ship builder—and around 1672, he was called the founder of *Beaubassin,* which for a time was known as *Bourgeoisville*.

The Blanchard and Bourgeois families were neighbors in *Belleisle* along the north side of the *Riviè*re Dauphin. On the 1671 Port Royal census, Jacques (Jacob) Bourgeois is listed with 20 *arpents* of cultivated land in two different locations. *Beaubassin* was probably the second location.

On the 1703 census, Anne Blanchard's sister, Marie, and her husband, Charles Bourgeois, were in *Beaubassin* with several children. On the same census, Anne Blanchard and Claude

Bourgeois are listed with one child, a girl. In all, Anne gave birth to 10 children: Marie, born in 1702; Paul, 1705; Claude, 1707; Joseph, 1709; Michel, 1711; Anne, 1718; Marguerite-Josephe, 1720; Olivier, 1723; Jean-Jacques, 1725; and Rosalie, born in 1732. Four girls and six boys.

All of the dates of birth are approximations. On one census record, the age of Anne and the age of her oldest child, if it is correct, would make mother Anne age eleven at the time of the child's birth. I also have my doubts about Rosalie, a possible last child of Anne's, born in 1732. That makes a 30-year span between the first and last child for Anne. I have Rosalie's name on my *Keep Checking* list.

Through the years in *Beaubassin*, the Acadians were trading with the people of Massachusetts and Quebec. There was no Maine or New Hampshire at this time. Massachusetts bordered on *Acadie*. New Hampshire became a state in 1788, and Maine in 1820. The Acadians were also trading with the people of other Acadian villages and the native Mi'kmaq. Boats were landing in *Beaubassin's* harbor and people were traveling overland through the area to other parts of *Acadie*.

In June of 1731, Robert Hale of Beverly, Massachusetts made a voyage to *Acadie* in the schooner, *Cupid,* and kept a journal. He was a medical doctor, born in 1703, and a graduate of Harvard College. He and the crew were bringing goods, plus 106 gallons of rum. In his diary, Hale calls *Beaubassin, Mesequesh,* the name of one of the rivers that runs from the village to the Bay of Fundy. On landing in *Beaubassin*, Hale wrote:

8 P.M. When wee came to our Boat (which wee left at high-water, wee found her aground near 1/4 of a Mile, but as the Shore was all descending, Muddy & very Soft & Slippery with our Guide's help wee made a Shift to Launch her, and it being by this Time young Flood wee put away for Mesequesh, a Small Village about 2 Leagues farther up the River, tho' indeed it is the largest in this Bay; but as it was now dark wee were obliged to keep in with the Shore lest wee shou'd miss the Crick, up which wee were to go abut 3/4 of a Mile to the Town; but the wind blowing very hard & right on upon the Shore, wee were put to much difficulty, & once got upon a

Rocky flat a considerable distance from the Shore where wee had like to have Stove our Boat to pieces, but at length wee espied the Creek and thrust our Boat in & soon had Smooth Water, & about 11 P.M. wee got up to the Town, to the House of one William Sears (Cyc sic) the Tavern Keeper, who let us in and gott water to wash our Legs & feet (bedaubed with Clay in coming ashore) & other Refreshments.

Hale, commenting on Acadian food, dress and housing:

There are but about 15 or 20 Houses in this Village, tho' it be the largest in the Bay, besides 2 Mass Houses or Churches, on one of which they hang out a Flagg Morning & Evening for Prayers, to the other the Priest goes once a day only; Habited like a Fool in Petticoats, with a Man after him with a Bell in one Hand ringing at every door, & a lighted Candle & Lanthorn in the other.

This Night wee lodg'd at Sear's again & at supper were regaled with Bonyclabber, soop, Sallet, roast Shad, & Bread & Butter, & to day wee din'd with M. Asneau at his Brother's upon roast Mutton, & for Sauce a Sallet, mix'd with Bonyclabber Sweetened with Molasses. Just about Bed time wee were surpriz'd to see some of ye Family on their Knees paying yt Devotions to ye Almighty , & others near them talking, & smoking & c. This they do all of the (mentally but not orally) every night & Morning, not altogether, but now one & then another & sometimes 2 or 3 together, but not in Conjunction one with the other. The women here differ as much in ye Cloathing (besides wearing of wooden Shoes) from those in New Engld as they do in Features & Complexion, wc is dark eno'by living in the Smoak in ye Summer to defend ymselves against Muskettoes, & in ye winter against ye Cold.

The Gait of ye pple is very different from ye English for the women Step (or rather straddle) further at a step than ye Men. The Women's Cloaths are good eno' fut they look as if they were pitched on with pitchforks, & very often yr Stockings are down about their heels.

They have but one Room in yr Houses besides a Cockloft, Cellar, & Sometimes a Closet. Their Bedrooms are made something after ye Manner of a Sailor's Cabbin, but boarded all round about yr bigness of ye Bed, except one little hole on the Foreside, just big eno' to crawl into before which is a Curtain drawn & as a Step to get into it, there stands a Chest. They have not above 2 or 3 chairs in a house, & those wooden ones, bottom & all. I saw but 2 Muggs among all ye French & ye lip of one of ym was broken down above 2 inches. When they treat you with strong drink they bring it in a large Bason & give you a Porringer to dip it with.

Hale's mindset of what's strange and different and his denigration of the culture and customs he observed are obvious. Many people quote his diary because it's available and quotable, but with objectivity and further reflection, his accounts, though they provide information on 18th-century Acadian life, also give a view of the biases and prejudices of some British colonialists.

Long before knowing I had ancestors who'd lived in *Beaubassin*, I stopped at a farm's yard sale on the edge of this sprawling marsh and bought an old Acadian dyke shovel. The owners were clearing everything out and moving away. There was still dirt on the shovel's metal, and the wooden handle was worn smooth from use. A while back, I looked in the darkest corner of our shed and found the old relic in a jumble of garden tools. The dirt was still on it, and everything else was as I remembered. A local friend told me that the shovels are called *ferrees* and were used well beyond Acadian times, so no telling how old mine is.

The Acadians at *Beaubassin* built their houses on high ridges away from the Bay of Fundy's winds and tides, which can rise as much as 50 feet—taller than a 3-story building. On each tide cycle, twice a day, 100 billion tons of seawater rises and recedes from the bottom of the Bay. There are days when the water is an iron oxide color from the churning sea, and the clouds above it reflect a pinkish hue.

Before I delved into the early years of my matriarchal line and learned some Acadian history, I only thought of my Cape Breton heritage. It's a revelation to know that I have ancestors who once lived in this isthmus where I am now. I've spent hours on their marsh, walking the dirt roads and paths, photographing the beauty of it, and painting the old marsh barns in a tone that shows them fading away.

Other artists have painted images of this magical place, and poets have praised its beauty. I've always felt a connection to this land, and now I know why. On this day, when I walked the marsh, taking in the panoramic view that sweeps through the grasses and sky, I stopped at the faded wood covered-bridge and watched a group of crows, perched like noisy sentinels on posts that line the narrow river below.

The Acadians called the marsh *Tintemarre* because of the racket or din of the birds and the ocean, and probably the wind. There are many birds on the marsh, and nearby, is an important feeding stop for migrating semipalmated sandpipers. The tiny (quiet) birds fly non-stop from the Arctic to this location to feed on the minuscule shrimp found in the mud flats during low tide. When the tides go out, a mile of shrimp-filled mud is exposed. The little birds remain in this area of the Dorchester Cape until they double their weight, then fly non-stop to Chile, where they winter. One day, while I was watching the beautiful movements of the sandpipers, a naturalist told me there were 500,000 birds out there. When the predator birds come close, the sandpipers lift off and fly close together, their bodies making grey colored waves moving gracefully in the sky — in the rhythm of a Viennese waltz.

For my Acadian people, the marsh they lived on was part of their migration, until they were driven out. On this day, looking at the sky, I saw swirling white clouds, moving, and creating shadows on the land. Both goodness and devastation occurred here for the Acadian people, but the clouds remind me of a moving on. I will myself not to get mired in the tragedy that occurred in this place, but to move on and see the totality of the Acadian journey.

My friend, Sylvia, has joined me on the marsh today. Walking is slow as we move off the paths and into the hip-high, wind-blown grasses that are swaying wildly. It's a gusty day. The crows and ravens are squawking, and Sylvia shouts that it's no wonder they called the place *Tintemarre*. The only things that are moving quietly are the newly built and elegant wind turbines that are harvesting energy nearby — standing like giant whirly-gigs in the clear blue sky.

Midway through the grasses, I dropped to my knees, then laid back, extending my arms to be in contact with as much of this earth as I could be. I stayed there a very long time and felt the power of the place, and the earth's coming to meet me. Reluctantly standing up, I moved in the direction of a monument in the marsh. There's something very lonely about it. Nearby, there's an Acadian flag and an Acadian cross.

Starting on the north side on the monument, first in French, then in English, it reads:

The Acadian Village
of Beaubassin on this site
was founded by
settlers from Port
Royal
around 1672
Upon the arrival of
Major Charles
Lawrence with British
troops in April 1750
the French authorities
Had the village destroyed
in order to force theAcadians to move to
the
French side of the
Missaguash River
Thus, Beaubassin
was
burned by Indians
likely under the
direction of Father
Germain and l'Abbe
Le Loutre

On the opposite side of the monument:

The inscribed names
are the last known
residents of
Beaubassin
in 1750, taken from
the
refugee list of 1751,
kept at the "Ministre
des colonies, depot des
papers publics des
colonies" in Paris
France

The writing disturbed me. Those who erected the monument made it sound so innocent, as if the English had little culpability in all that happened here.

I tried to let the frustration go, walked to the west side of the monument, and found two names out of the 52 inscribed that leapt out at me:

Claude Bourgeois and Anne Blanchard
and higher up,

Francois Arseneau and Anne Bourgeois.

The two Annes—mother and daughter. My third and fourth grandmothers, with their husbands. The power of seeing their names chiseled in stone jolted me. Until then, I'd only encountered them on paper, on the internet, or walked on their land. I stepped back to the meadow and picked a handful of wild flowers growing there. Then, with some of the grasses, I circled the flower stems together and placed the little bouquet on the stone beneath their names.

I looked again at the listing of the last people living in Beaubassin before the village was burned, before the Acadian villages in all other parts of *Acadie* were burned, before deportations, and thought about all the children who were caught up in the political upheaval. They are not mentioned. Not inscribed on the monument are the children of Anne Bourgeois and Francois Arseneau, and all the other children of the village who were also among the last people living in *Beaubassin*—their young lives uprooted, and maybe cut short by *le Grande Dérangement.*

The Last Inhabitants

Pierre Deraier and Francoise Arsenau
Jaques Mouton and Marguerite Kessy
Francois Arsenau and Anne Bourgeois
Abraham Arsenau and Agnes Sire
Marie Sire
Pierre Gravois and Marie Rose Bourgeois
Francoise Sire
Jaques Bourgeois and Marie Bourque
Pierre Arsenau and Jeanne Marie Heon
Marie Chiasson
Claude Bourgeois and Anne Blanchard
Michel Bourgeois and Marie Doucet
Charles Heon and Marie Jeanne Bourgeois
Jean Kessy and Marie Richard
Paul Sire
Oliver Bourgeois

# of Beaubassin

Pierre Cottard amd Agnes Bourgeois
Jean Mouton and Marguerite Poirier
Baptise Bourgeois and Anne Bernard
Claude Bourgeois
Michel Poirier and Madeline Bourgeois
Francois Bourel and Marguerite Doucet
Claude Tendon and Francoise Kessy
Claude Poirier and Marguerite Sire
Marie Kessy
Paul Devau and Marguerite Buote
Vincent Devau and Marie Buote
Claude Kessy and Anne Chiasson
Jaques Kessy and Marie Olivier
Joseph Arsenau
Anne Buote
Jean Arseneau
Brele and Anne Sire

Anne (dite Annette) Bourgeois

Born
1718, Beaubassin, Acadie

Died
unknown

Daughter of
Anne Blanchard
b. 1682, Port Royal, Acadie
d. Unknown
Claude Bourgeois
b. 1674, Port Royal, Acadie
d. Unknown

Spouse
Francois (dit petit) Arseneau,
b. 1710, Beaubassin, Acadie
d. Unknown

Son of
Anne Boudrot
b. 1679, Oisiguit, Acadie
d. unknown
Pierre Arsenault
b. 1679, Acadie
d. unknown

I think about Anne Blanchard, Annette Bourgeois, and their families, wondering how much they witnessed as their homes and crops were burning. What happened to their livestock? In 1750, Annette and Petit Francois Arseneau had five children, ages 3 to 10 years old. Were the children moved to another location before the village turned to ash—the smoke visible, the smell acrid from wherever they were?

The upheaval on the narrow isthmus of *Chignecto*, which played a major role in the preliminaries to the expulsion of thousands of Acadians, is difficult to imagine. Noise on the *Tintemarre* Marsh was no longer just the natural sounds of ducks and geese flying over the peaceful fields. Instead, there were troops arriving and the sounds of gunfire.

There have been entire books written about the causes and tragedies of this turbulent time period in *Acadie*. Conflicts between England and France, the Acadians' wish to remain neutral, their refusal to sign a loyalty oath to the King of England, the parts their priests played, the roles of the Mi'kmaq, forts built and taken, raids, retaliations, and in the end, in 1750, *Beaubassin* was burned to the ground. Only it was the beginning—the start of deportations, deaths, and more destruction.

Many say it was more than just power struggles between France and England (including troops from the New England colony). It was also about religion, trade, and ethnic cleansing.

Those living in *Beaubassin*, and later, those all over *Acadie*, lost their land, their livestock, their possessions, their livelihood. The people of *Acadie* were put on boats and sent first to the 13 American colonies controlled by Britain. After 1758, families were deported to France and England. Some historians have estimated that perhaps as many as 11,000 people were deported and that one third of them died from disease or drowning during the frightful journeys. Families were separated, and many were imprisoned in Halifax and in England. They were dispersed along the coast of America, from Massachusetts to Georgia. More than a thousand Acadians first sent to Virginia, then put back on ships and taken to England.

Some were deported to the West Indies and died there.

Many people went by boat across the Northumberland Strait to *Ile-Saint-Jean,* (today's Prince Edward Island). Though the Treaty of Utrecht established England's dominance and established the Acadians as British subjects, *Ile-Saint-Jean* was still under French control, and some of those fleeing capture by the British had relatives living on the Island. But in 1758, both *Ile-Saint-Jean* and *Ile-Royale* (Cape Breton Island) were cleared of Acadians. Great numbers were taken to France, and three of the ships making the long voyage across the Atlantic sank. From this tragedy, it's estimated that 850 lives were lost.

The large movement of Acadians settling in Louisiana started in 1764 when 20 of those who had been sent to New York originally, traveled south. In 1764-65, about 311 people arrived in Louisiana from Halifax, and 689 came from both Pennsylvania and Maryland from 1766 to 1770. In 1785 nearly 1,600 Acadians who had been deported to France returned to North America to settle in Louisiana—and 19 came from *St. Pierre* in 1788—all numbers that can be found in records for this time. The people now called *Cajuns* have a strong identity in their Louisiana home, and have developed their own unique culture. From my research, I see some of the Acadian names I'm most familiar with among the groups of people who went to Louisiana, but none of my direct ancestors moved there.

On July 11, 1764, the British passed an order that Acadians could return to their former homeland only if they signed an unconditional oath of allegiance to the King of England. The census of that year showed that during all of the years of deportation, only 2,600 Acadians had eluded capture and remained in *Acadie*. Those who escaped deportation spent years of continually moving from place to place, in hiding, and in near destitution—struggling to survive. For those who were deported, the inhabitants in most of the places where they were first sent did not want them and gave them little help. Reports of their treatment, isolation, and rejections are difficult to read.

I telephoned Stephen White at the *Centre d'études acadiennes* to find out what happened to Anne Blanchard and Claude Bourgeois, and to Annette Bourgeois and Petit Francois

Arseneau. I wanted to know about my family. Were they deported or imprisoned? I know they survived because next in my matrilineal line is Annette and Francois' child, Apolline, my fifth grandmother. But where did the family go during the years of turmoil. How did they remain alive? I also wanted to ask about the treatment the Acadians received. It was bad enough that they were deported, but I asked Stephen, "Why did so many places reject them?"

"You must remember that there were no social services then," he said. "There were no public funds to be used to help. When the Acadians were dropped off in communities in the American colonies, in England, even in France, they arrived with nothing and needed everything. They were farmers and their livestock and lands had been taken away from them. The skilled tradesmen had no tools. Some were fishermen and their boats and gear were gone. They were a burden on the communities they escaped to, or were deported to. The inhabitants of these locations didn't want them, and didn't want to support them. Sometimes they drove them out, or left them hungry and hurting."

Stephen White told me that for many families, no information has been found, and if Acadians escaped deportation, it's common that there is no record of them anywhere.

"But we have information about your family," he said. "We've been able to track Francois (*dit petite*) Arseneau and Ann (*dite* Annette) Bourgeois. After the burning of Beaubassin, the couple and their children and Anne's parents are all found on the census in Baie Verte on the Northumberland Strait. Annette and Francois and their children are also found later on the *Miquelon* census."

The enumerations in the 1752 census of the Acadian region, two years after the burning of Beaubassin, are different than any census in previous years. Many of the settlements around the burned-out Beaubassin are listed—but in most places, the people are divided into two groups—inhabitants and refugees. Exceptions to this are *Gaspareaux* (a French fort), *Portage* (the route between *Beaubassin* and *Baie Verte*), *Pont Buot* (*Point de Bute*), and *Baie Verte*. They all show refugees only. There were 23 refugee families in *Baie Verte* in 1752, and listed among them are Claude Bourgeois and his wife, Ann Blanchard, and Francois Arseneau, his wife, Annette (Anne) Bourgeois, with one boy and five girls (no names or ages for the children are given).

The word *refugees* catches in my throat whenever I say it. Situations similar to the Acadians' plight are still happening all over the world today. Whether caused by ethnic cleansing, wars, or persecution, whole groups of people are being driven out, or dispersed— dying in the face of the turmoil, living their lives in refugee camps, or on the move, looking for a place to be safe and start anew.

Although my family has never been found on any documents on *Isle Saint Jean* (now Prince Edward Island), many Acadians did go there after the burning of *Beaubassin*, swelling the population from around 700 to approximately 3,000 soon after the Expulsion activities in the region began. The name Arseneau is common on Prince Edward Island. One of its early settlers was an Arseneau, and I wonder if Francois and Annette might have moved their family across the waters of the Northumberland Strait during the time when it was still under French control, thinking it would be a safe haven with relatives. Based on what is known of the movements of this family, it seemed logical to speculate that they either owned a boat capable of sailing across the waters that they crossed, or they had access to one.

After the *Baie Verte* refugee census list, the next time Annette and Francois are cited is in the 1767 census listing of the island of *Miquelon*. The Islands of *Saint Pierre* and *Miquelon* are 12 miles from the coast of Newfoundland, close to the Grand Banks, famous for its fishing. They belong to France though they're 2,000 miles from the French shore. Stephen White told me that Annette Bourgeois and Francois Arseneau and their children (and many others) were eventually expelled from *St. Pierre et Miqelon* because they were Acadian, not considered to be French by the local authorities.

Confirming the speculation that they had a boat to travel on, Stephen White showed me documentation that a ship called *Deux Amie* (Two Friends) left the island of *Miquelon* on the 6th of October, 1767, with 35 people on board. Francois Arseneau and Annette Bourgeois were on the ship—listed first on the manifest, so Francois probably was the ship's owner. The couple's children were also on board, and all of the remaining passengers with them were connected to Anne and Francois by blood or by marriage. It's uplifting to think of them being together and how fortunate it was that they had a seaworthy vessel large enough to accommodate them all.

There were three ships travelling together leaving *Miquelon* on that October day—the *Deux Amie*, carrying 35 people, the *Maryanne* with 28, and an unnamed vessel with 30 passengers. There were also five shallops, which are large dories that usually carry three or four people. The Acadians on these ships were forced to leave *Miquelon* and were promised passage to France, but instead, they chose to return to *Acadie*.

After the family's expulsion from *Michelon*, there is a gap of time with no official information about them, until a record of Francois (Petit) Arseneau is found in *Caraquet* in present day New Brunswick, where he is buried. There are no records of the death of Annette Bourgeois, or of her parents, Anne Blanchard and Claude Bourgeois.

Stephen White also mentioned that there are documents referring to Francois and his brother applying to the authorities for permission to operate a boat service to the *Îles de la Madeleine*. These islands are in the Gulf of St. Lawrence and can be reached by ferry from Souris, on Prince Edward Island. (Souris was founded by Acadians in 1727, and was overrun by field mice at one time—hence the name *Souris*, meaning *mouse* in French). Today, the *Îles de la Madeleine* belong to the Province of Quebec, but the archipelago is closer to Prince Edward Island (105 kilometers) and Cape Breton Island (85 kilometers away) than it is to Quebec.

On a painting trip to Parrsboro, Nova Scotia, I went to the Genealogy Center at the Ottawa House beside Partridge Island and found some literature mentioning a Francois (they call him Francis) Arseneau and Jean, (they call him John) Bourg, two Acadians who were allowed to stay in the area after the Expulsion because they were operating a much needed ferry service from Partridge Island across the Minas Basin in the Bay of Fundy to Blomidon Island.

Steven White emailed me the information that in 1764, according to the *Public Archives of*

Nova Scotia, and cited in the book, *Les Acadiens avant 1755*, François Arseneau and his son-in-law Jean Bourg obtained permission to run a ferry from Partridge Island.

The Bay of Fundy crossing between Partridge Island and Blomidon is the narrowest part of the Basin, providing an obvious ferry link to other parts of the mainland. The Mi'kmaq called Partridge Island *Wa'so'q*, meaning *Heaven*, because it was a place for gathering amethyst, which they considered to be sacred. Some people say it's also called *Grandmother's Cooking Pot*, because twice a day, when air that's trapped in holes on the Island's basalt is pushed out as the tide rises, the water appears to be bubbling and boiling.

When I checked back with Stephen White about the story of Francois and Jean Bourg operating a ferry, he told me that this is confusing because he has found an official British military record that kept track of the number of Acadians in the area and where they were located. That record states that Francois Arseneau was operating a boat service on a river in *Baie Verte* on the Northumberland Strait.

Nowadays, I find that on nearly any kind of excursion I take, I add on a genealogy stop. When we booked theatre tickets at the Ship's Company in Parrsboro, we left home early so I could go to the Genealogy Center and revisit the subject of Francois and a possible ferry business before the evening performance was scheduled to begin. At the Center, I gently asked the genealogists if there were original source materials regarding Francois Arseneau and Jean Bourg operating a ferry service from Partridge Island to Blomidon.

"How shall I write about this?" I ask.

"It's simple," I'm told. "Just say your source is from the Parrsboro Genealogical Society."

And so, I'm left to wonder whether Francois (dit petit) operated a ferry service from Partridge Island to Blomidon, or engaged in some sort of business on a river in *Baie Verte*, nearly 84 kilometers (by road) away. But most importantly, Annette and Francois and their extended family stayed safe during the upheaval—wherever they were.

Le Grand Dérangement is a terrible chapter in human history. It's with profound sadness that I read about the death and destruction that came to so many families. And with enormous gratitude I learn of the lives spared in my own family. Although my ancestors suffered many ordeals and uprootings, theirs was a fortunate outcome—they remained alive and went on within their culture in *Acadie*.

At the turn of this century, around 2001, the *Sociéte Nationale de l'Acadie* requested an apology from the British Government regarding *Le Grand Dérangement*. "We want England to accept that this was an unacceptable act," said society president Euclide Chiasson. "It was an ethnic cleansing, and some people are still denying it." Negotiations took place for two years and in 2003, it was announced that the queen's representative in Canada would sign an officially sanctioned acknowledgment of responsibility. It read:

Whereas on 28 July 1755, the Crown, in the course of administering the affairs of the British colony of Nova Scotia, made the decision to deport the Acadian people;

Whereas the deportation of the Acadian people, commonly known as le Grand Dérangement, continued until 1763 and had tragic consequences, including the deaths of many thousands of Acadians - from disease, in shipwrecks, in their places of refuge and in prison camps in Nova Scotia and England as well as in the British colonies in America;

Whereas We acknowledge these historical facts and the trials and suffering experienced by the Acadian people during le Grand Dérangement;

Whereas We hope that the Acadian people can turn the page on this dark chapter of their history;

.....Now know you that we, by and with the advice of Our Privy Council for Canada, do by this Our Proclamation..... designate 28 July of every year as "A Day of Commemoration of the Great Upheaval," commencing on 28 July 2005.

The *Sociéte Nationale de l'Acadie* was enthusiastic to receive the news of the Royal Proclamation. It was a statement of facts, no more denying on England's behalf.

But there is no apology. Perhaps powerful nations do not apologize.

Though many questions are left unanswered regarding Annette Bourgeois and Petit Francois

Arseneau, I do know that they had eight children: Marie Madeleine, b.1740; Pierre, b.1742; Anne (Nanon), b.1743; Marguerite, b.1745; Henriette, b.1747; Anastasie, b.1754; Anne Adelaide, b.1757, and Apolline, born in 1760. Seven girls and one boy.

Anne was 22 when her first child was born and 42 when she gave birth to Apolline. The first five children were born before the burning of *Beaubassin* and the family's forced exit. The last baby born before the village burning was Henriette in 1747. Then, for seven years there were no family births. During the time of this gap, they were moving, searching for safe havens, and facing dangerous situations. I've also seen one report stating that Francois was captured by the British and put in the prison on George's Island in Halifax harbor for a period of time.

After the seven-year period of time with no family births, Anne's sixth child, Anastasie, was born in 1754, followed three years later by Adelaide in 1757, then Apolline in 1760.

Apolline, Anne's last child, is my fifth grand-mother. I'm intrigued by her name, by all the children's names, and wonder who in the family did the melodic child-naming.

I imagine Anne, standing by the door, watching the children playing in a distant field. She's calling out to them—and their names create a beautiful song.

Madeleine…Pierre…
Marguerite…Henriette…
Anastasie…Adelaide…
Nanon…and…Apolline……..

Apolline Arseneau

Born

1760, unknown, while the family were refugees

Died

1827, Cheticamp, Cape Breton Island

Daughter of

Anne Bourgeois
b.1718, Beaubassin
d. unknown
Francois (dit Petit) Arseneau
b.1739, Acadie
d. unknown

Spouse

Jean Francois Regis Bois
b.1766, Port Toulouse, Cape Breton Island
d. before January 7,1822, not at daughter's wedding

Son of

Jeanne Dugas
b.1731
d. after 1817,
when she was interviewed by the Bishop
Pierre Bois
b.1733
d. after 1791

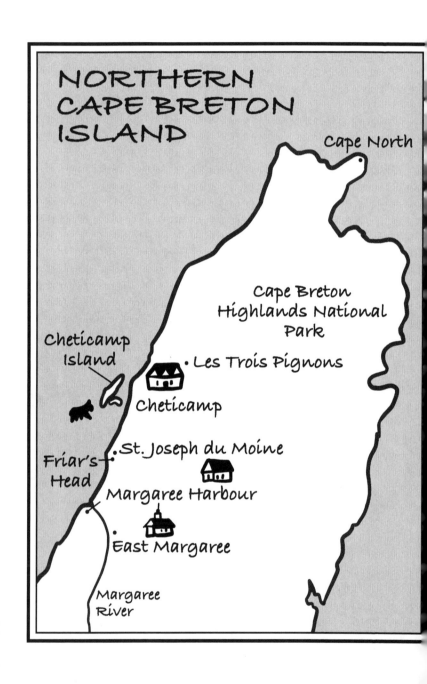

NORTHERN CAPE BRETON ISLAND

Cape North

Cape Breton Highlands National Park

Cheticamp Island

Les Trois Pignons

Cheticamp

St. Joseph du Moine

Friar's Head

Margaree Harbour

East Margaree

Margaree River

I spent a lot of time wondering about Apolline. She was seven years old and the youngest member of her refugee family on the first documentation of her that I located — the 1767 census on the island of *Miquelon*, belonging to France, though it's off the coast of Newfoundland. The next time I found her was on the 1809 Cheticamp, *Ile Royale* (Cape Breton) census — the oldest enumeration of that area that's been found. Apolline is listed there with her husband, Jean Francois Regis Bois, and their three daughters — Marie-Madeleine, Genevieve, and Hélène.

Apolline and Regis were living in *le Platin*, an area running parallel to the sea, but tucked behind a ridge, keeping them out of sight of anyone on the water. After the years of hiding or being captured by people arriving by sea, most early Cheticamp families chose to live where they weren't visible from the ocean.

There's a cemetery in *le Platin* sitting on a hilltop, hidden by stands of trees and unruly brush. By the road, a large stone with an inscription reads, *1 ER CIMETIERE DES 14 VIEUX* — then below, *OLD CEMETERY*. The path up to the graveyard is narrow and curves through ground cover and wild flowers. At the top of the hill, the path widens to reveal the sacred space. The area is completely surrounded by graceful trees and is the gentlest graveyard I've ever been in. The grass is just long enough to lend a feeling of softness, and scattered around, a few delicate clover lean their heads against the sandstone graves. In uneven rows, the stone markers connect to the ground as though they've grown there. They're humble, and there's a unity about the place. No gravestone stands out as better or more important than any other. On my visit, I didn't single out any marker, or spend time searching for names. I felt connected to them all and stayed for a while.

In a peaceful state of mind, I left the *Cimetiere des 14 Vieux* and wound my way back down the path and across the country road. There, a tall monument memorializes the 14 founders of Cheticamp:

Pierre Bois, Peter Aucoin, Joseph Boudrot, Joseph Godet, Paul Chiasson, Bazile Chiasson, Joseph Desveaux, Gregoire Maliette, Jean Chiasson, Lazare White, Raymond Poirier, Anselm Aucoin, Joseph (Aucoin) and Justin Desveaux.

These are the men who signed the petition (some, by placing an *X*) to acquire land and create their villages.

Many men did not come to Cheticamp alone. Women came with them, taking risks, bearing children, and turning structures into homes. After all the post-deportation years of wandering from place to place and trying to seek safety and stability for themselves and their children, the women helped make Cheticamp into a community, where they could once again sink down Acadian roots. Standing by the monument, I felt the need to remember—and champion the women who also came here—and remember the

199

important roles they played in the founding and preserving of Cheticamp and all other Acadian communities.

Pierre Bois, listed first on the monument, is the father of Apolline's husband, Jean Francois Regis Bois. Pierre, his wife Jeanne Dugas, and their children came to Cheticamp around 1782, one of the first families to arrive. It's unknown when Apolline Arseneau, who married their son, Regis, came to Cheticamp, but it may have been with a group from *Ile St. Jean* (Prince Edward Island) that included several Arseneau and Chiasson families.

After the Treaty of Paris was signed in 1763, France relinquished to England the ownership of most of its holdings in North America. In the 1770s, the Nova Scotia government encouraged the resettlement of Acadians by guaranteeing land grants, freedom of worship for Catholics, and a promise that there would be no further expulsions. Some of the surviving Acadians who were deported to places outside of *Acadie*, chose to stay where they were sent, others returned to Nova Scotia, and about 1,500 made their way from the American colonies, Nova Scotia, and France to Louisiana. The people who had always stayed in hiding, or were in prison in Nova Scotia, started to live more freely and were allowed to re-establish themselves, but not in Port Royal or Grand-Pré.

All of the Acadian dyked lands were now occupied by Loyalists who came to British Nova Scotia after England lost to the colonists in the American Revolution. Eight thousand New England Planters, about 2,000 families, took up the offer of Nova Scotia's Governor Lawrence's urging to come and settle on the deported Acadian lands. Fishermen and their families responded to the Governor's advertisement in the *Boston Gazette* on October 12, 1758, and again on January 11, 1759. They were promised 100 acres and another 50 acres for each member of the family—up to 1,000 acres. The fishermen received as much land as the farmers, and since they were already fishing off the Nova Scotia coast, it was an especially appealing offer.

The attraction for the farmers who came was that most of them were poor, and there was a scarcity of land in New England.

The Acadians who wanted to stay in Nova Scotia had to go to infertile and isolated places to begin anew. Between 1758 and 1783, Catholics (which meant Acadians) were not allowed to own land in Nova Scotia. After 1764, they could only hold land that had been set aside for them as tenants, and until 1804, they could not legally reside outside of these lands.

As the number of families who came to Cheticamp grew, a group of men organized to seek property. Pierre Bois is the first of those listed in the charter document who went to Sydney (Nova Scotia), petitioning for land in 1790. This group, memorialized on the stone across from the old *le Platin* cemetery, is known as *Les Quatorze Vieux* (The Fourteen Old Ones). The original settlers, even though they were not old in years at the time of their prominence, have always been labeled *Vieux*.

The group of 14 obtained a government charter granting them 7,000 acres of land, mainly in *Petit-Étang, Le Platin, Plateau,* and *Pointe-á-la-Croix.* According to Anselm Chiasson in his book, *Cheticamp,* the original land charter and those that followed did not assign lots to individuals. Instead, they left it up to the petitioners to parcel out the acreage. The best locations were dealt with immediately, and the rest at later dates. Among the 7,000 acres, there were areas of land designated for communal use—a large space identified for gardens, for instance. Another area was set aside for the collection of seaweed, and there's a directive for the use of the maple tree stands.

On the Northumberland Strait, where we live, one elderly neighbor always gathered seaweed each fall and banked the foundation of his house with it, in preparation for winter. I wonder if the Cheticamp Acadians did the same thing. It was fascinating to watch our neighbor, choosing the same area by the tidal river to collect the seaweed, raking it in, pulling it away from the high tide line to spread it out to dry, then with his well-worn rake, collecting the dried seaweed together in order to take it home in a trailer pulled behind his old black Chevy. The whole process lasted a week or two, and once he collected a large pile, he'd put in stakes around the house foundation, and pack in his insulation from the sea. Some people here also spread seaweed on their gardens for fertilizer. Charlie Dan, from *Trois Pignons*, tells me that his father would never use seaweed to nourish his crops, "because it made bad potatoes." I've heard that said in our area, too.

Once, on Prince Edward Island's northwest shore, I watched as men with draft horses gathered in Irish Moss, a kind of seaweed, from the ocean. The powerful horses were hitched to giant barrel-sized rakes they pulled behind, and the men rode them into the sea, maneuvering the animals, and letting the claws of the rake catch the seaweed floating in the crashing waves. When the huge rakes were full, they'd steer the horses to shore, dump their *catch*, load it onto truck beds, and drive it to fields where they'd spread the moss to dry.

Watching the men and horses working in the sea made me feel I'd stepped back a hundred years—or into something surreal. The working men looked like seafaring cowboys. "Notice how much fun it looks like they're having—horses, too," a local woman said as we watched. "Like they're enjoying a day at the beach." And I agreed, but wondered how the *cowboys* and horses would respond to that observation. In other parts of the world where this kind of seaweed is gathered, workers pick it off rocks, but the harvesters of Prince Edward Island let a churning sea help them in their task.

Besides mentioning seaweed in the designations for land use in Cheticamp's common areas, there was also concern for the protection and ownership of the stands of maple trees. History suggests that the Acadians learned to make maple syrup and maple sugar from the Mi'kmaq, and, clearly, they valued the trees that provided the sap to make the sweet tasting liquid and granules.

The 14 men who petitioned the government in 1790 were trying to regain something they had before the Deportation—land to live and work on. As a condition of the grant, the families had to agree that they would clear a portion of their holding, put up buildings, keep farm animals, and cultivate a designated amount of acreage. But land on Cape Breton Island was not destined to become fertile farmland. And it's not marshland to dyke. It's rocky and of poor quality. The Acadians attended to the requirements of the grant, but to meet the material needs of their families, they fished. Cod (*la morue*) was the principle catch, and fishermen, mostly from other countries, had been involved in the catching of it for centuries.

During the week, most of the men in Cheti-camp lived in fishing cabins near the harbor. They were working for the Robin Company, which was based in the British Channel Island of Jersey, but running fishing operations in the Gaspé, Arichat, and Cheticamp. On weekends, the men traveled home to be with their families—their houses were too far away from the sea for daily commutes to and from the fishing operation. According to geneologist Charlie Dan Roach, each man brought food to cook, and probably to share with cabinmates. The most popular dish was a one-pot meal of freshly-caught fish and vegetables (probably potatoes) cooked together. It makes me think of the Acadian chowder I learned how to make from the animated waitress at the Cheticamp Co-op restaurant.

I imagine the men, after a full day of fishing, and then their meal (with little cleanup since it was just one pot), smoking and having a little of the rum they bought from the Robins company store.

The wives would be home, taking care of the children, tending the garden, the house, the chickens, and the other animals. They would also be helping one another in the spirit of community that the Acadians lived in. They usually had female family connections nearby to support them in their daily work.

From the 1809 Cheticamp census, I see that Apolline's brother, Pierre Arseneau, with his wife, Marie LeBlanc, and nine children were living in nearby Margaree. Apolline's sister Marguerite, married to Basile Cormier, was also in Margaree, with no children listed, and their sister Anne, married to Basile Chiasson, was living on Cheticamp Island with their four children.

On Apolline's husband's side of the family, Regis' sister, Genevieve Bois, married to Maximin Godet, and with six children, lived close by in *Le Platin.*

Jeanne Dugas, Apolline's mother-in-law, was listed as a widow in 1809, living next to Regis, Apolline and their three daughters. Jeanne was an important woman in the region and now, in history. For most of her life, she was a midwife and healer. Midwives played a crucial role in their community, especially in one having as many babies as the Acadian women had. Infant mortality was low, and the Acadian people in general had long lifespans. The first doctor came to Cheticamp in 1875, and in the years before that, the community relied on midwives as healers, and practitioners with locally grown remedies. Midwives could also baptize infants when the situation was urgent and there were no priests around.

Visits by priests to the isolated areas around Cheticamp were rare. It was so cut off from population centers and regular church services that the people relied on midwives and church-designated elders to carry out the sacraments they adhered to. The people the priests designated as elders were given the authority to stand in for them, and were held in high regard in their community. The same held true for midwives.

In 2016, Parks Canada recognized Jeanne Dugas, Apolline's mother-in-law, as a Person of National Historic Significance, writing in part:

Dugas and other Acadian women in this time period ensured the survival of their families and communities, thus contributing to the survival of the Acadian people. Throughout the privations and instability of war, Dugas managed to feed and care for her family, and she helped rebuild her family's life in new and unfamiliar locations. In Cheticamp, Dugas worked as the village midwife, and as midwives were also caregivers, she likely looked after the sick. In this role, she helped her community flourish during the years of Acadian resettlement in Cape Breton after 1764.

Jeanne Dugas also stands as a mirror of the Acadian experience during the Deportation era. In 1812, Bishop Plessis, during his visit to

Chéticamp, wrote:

Worthy of note is that I met at Chéticamp, on Cape Breton Island, in July of 1812, Jeanne Dugast, aged about 80 years then, the widow of Pierre Bois, who told me she had been born in Louisbourg (Cape Breton), and later, of living on Ilse St-Jean (P.E.I.), after that at Remshic, in Acadia, thence again to Cape Breton, from there again to Remshic, then to Ile St-Jean a second time, then a third time to Remshic, from there to Restigouche, from Restigouche to Halifax, from there to Arichat, then to the Magdalen Islands, then to Cascapédia, and from Cascapédia to Chéticamp, and of never going to bed without supper.

Apolline remains, in many ways, a mystery to me. She was not (statistically) a typical Acadian woman. She married, at age 35, a man six years younger than she was, and she had only three children—Marie-Madeleine, Genevieve, and Hélène.

The first of Apolline's daughters, Marie-Madeleine Bois, is my fourth grandmother, and for entirely different reasons, she, too, was definitely not a typical Acadian woman. That's something she may have learned from her mother, Apolline, and her grandmother, Jeanne Dugas.

Marie Madeleine Bois

Born
1794, Cheticamp, Cape Breton Island

Died
1884, Cheticamp, Cape Breton Island

Daughter of
Apolline Arsenault
b.1760, unknown, refugee
d. 1827, Cheticamp, Cape Breton Island
Jean Francois Regis Bois,
b.1766, Port Toulouse, Cape Breton Island
d. unknown

Spouse
Hubert Aucoin
b.1791, Cheticamp, Cape Breton Island
d. about.1832, at sea
Son of
Rose Marie Chiasson,
b.1764
d.1852
Anselme Aucoin
b.1763
d.1824

My final afternoon of looking for information about Marie Madeleine Bois was one disappointment followed by many others. After repeatedly entering into the computer what little I knew about her in every possible search variation I could think of, I continued to come up with nothing new to aid me in my search.

I had her date and place of birth, and her marriage to Hubert Aucoin was well documented. On Sunday, July 25, 1812, at *L'Eglise Saint Pierre* in Cheticamp, the Bishop of Quebec, Joseph-Octave Plessis officiated at the marriage of six couples from Cheticamp and Margaree:

Charles Boudrot and Luce Aucoin, André Poirier and Anastasie Deveaux, Frédéric Deveaux and Marguerite Romard, and Hubert Aucoin and Marie Madeleine Bois, along with two couples from Margaree, Paul Doucet and Marthe Haché, and Jean Etchevery and Henriette Larade. The July date was a busy time for sacraments. Two priests accompanying Bishop Plessis performed 17 baptisms that same day.

Both Hubert Aucoin and Charles Boudrot were able to sign their names on their marriage certificates. It was well known in the community that the two of them could write (at least their names) and they were often called on to witness legal documents. At the time of the wedding, these two men were the only ones, other than the dignitaries, who placed a signature on any certificates. There were no schools in Cheticamp then, and most of the people were illiterate. Fortunately, they had a rich oral history which was honored and passed down through the generations to help us know something of them. We also have census information and other civil documents available.

While researching Marie Madeleine and Hubert, I also found multiple references to the disappearance and presumed death of Hubert. Oral history, and now written accounts, tell of a shipwreck near an island between Nova Scotia and Newfoundland, called *Ile Saint-Paul*. Hubert's wreck happened at a point where the Atlantic Ocean and the Gulf of Saint Lawrence meet, and because of the convergence, the winds and weather there can change quickly, making it dangerous for sailors, and giving the area the reputation as the *Graveyard of the Gulf.*

Secondary sources about Hubert Aucoin report that he was probably the captain of a boat that left on a seal hunt with other men on several other vessels. The sealers from Cheticamp usually began their hunt once the ice started to thaw and break-up, and the men usually all went out to sea at the same time. When they came back from the hunt, Hubert and his crew were not among them, and were never seen again.

It's assumed that the sealing boat was broken up by ice, and the crew was lost, but the story tells that Hubert must have clung to an ice floe that brought him to land on *Ile Saint-Paul.* The accounts go on to say that many years later, a sailor landing on *Ile Saint-Paul.* found bones and an inscription which read:

Hubert Aucoin, son of Anselme Aucoin, dead from hunger and thirst. If you find my body, please bury it.

If the tale is true, and the sailor who found the bones buried them, then came back to report the finding to Marie Madeleine and her family, hopefully, it could have brought them some measure of closure. There were many years between Hubert's actual disappearance and the story's description of a sailor's discovery. But I wonder—could the sailor read?

Equally sad, but without an accompanying narrative is the report that Marie Madeleine's son, Norbert, on April 5th, 1842, also drowned at sea.

Although I knew of the sea tragedies and the significance of their well-documented wedding, I continued to search for information about Marie Madeleine. Well into time spent with no results, I thought of the whole issue of changing and misspelling names. *Bois* and Marie *Madeleine* or *Magdeleine* were unlikely to be the problem, but Hubert's Aucoin surname could be. I suddenly remembered Nelly's neighbor on her porch in Newton, the woman who spoke the same patois French as the others—Mrs. O'Quin. And a woman at the Aucoin reunion had told me about variations of their name, so I changed tactics. Besides entering Marie Madeleine and Hubert together, plus their Cheticamp location, and the word Acadian, I tried misspelling the Aucoin name. And on what could have been the last chance of finding anything about the elusive Marie Madeleine, I used O'Quin—and found a Google listing for *The Widow of Hubert O'Quin.*

The entry was on the personal blog of Robert Campbell, a professor from the University of Cape Breton in Sydney, Nova Scotia. He was doing research on the Phillip Robin Company. Its owners were from the Isle of Jersey, off the British coast, and they were running multiple fishing operations in Canada from 1765 to 1955. Their first location was in Quebec, the second in Arichat (where the Boudrots had settled) and the third was in Cheticamp. The Robin Company was the reason Pierre Bois, one of the original Acadian settlers of Cheticamp, and Marie Madeleine's father-in-law, with his family, moved to Cheticamp.

From Robert Campbell's blog, I learned Robin operated the company on a *truck economy*. The use of the term comes from the French word, *troquer* — to exchange or barter. *Wikipedia* goes on to explain:

A truck system differs from this kind of open barter or payment in kind system by creating or taking advantage of a closed economic system in which workers have little or no opportunity to choose other work arrangements, and can easily become so indebted to their employers that they are unable to leave the system legally.

Under the truck economy, an individual's debt was recorded in a ledger book, and when that person gave fish or services to the Robin Company, credit was given to them. The individual's credit could also be transferred to someone else's account, and debt or credit was carried over from one year's books to the next.

The Robin Company established the value of goods the Acadians bought from the company store, and the prices the company would pay for fish the Acadians delivered to them (freshly-caught or cured, inferior grade to top quality). There was no other store in or anywhere near Cheticamp, so the Acadians had to buy from and sell to the Robin Company. The situation reminds me of the Merle Travis song, *Sixteen Tons*, about a coal miner who tells Saint Peter, *Don't you call me 'cause I can't go. I owe my soul to the company store.*

In Professor Campbell's blog, he wrote that in the 1843 Robin Company ledger, there's an account for the widow of Hubert O'Quin. He only identifies her in this way, and continues on, explaining that a widow with an account is not surprising. In any year during this time period there were usually about 400 accounts—a dozen of them being widows who made few purchases. The widow of Hubert O'Quin, surprisingly, had an unusually large account compared to all of the 400 accounts (male and female) in the ledgers.

Often in the past, I've begun reading information about a potential ancestor, only to find as I continued, that it wasn't a person in my direct line after all. The Acadians baptized their babies using a small number of first names, and frequently, if a child died, the parents gave the deceased's name to a later-born baby. Also, within the population, there were not a lot of different surnames. In Cheticamp, around this date, Aucoin, LeBlanc, and Chiasson were the most common names.

Robert Campbell resolved the issue of the use of the name *O'Quin* — determining that the Jersey men of the Robin Company used that spelling, instead of the correct *Aucoin* when they entered transactions for any members of this family. He also did a genealogical search, confirming that Marie Madeleine Bois was the widow of Hubert Aucoin, and linked them both to their parents, according to the same information that I had. What a find this blog entry was! I was thrilled to have the personal facts verified, and finished reading it, assured that the information was about my fourth grandmother.

In the last paragraph of Robert Campbell's blog entry, he turned his attention to the Robin Company ledgers of *The Widow of Hubert O'Quin*, and wrote:

Tracking entries of Marie-Madeleine both before and after 1843, it turns out that she was actually widowed in 1831, her husband leaving her with a debt of about 37 pounds, and she is still on the books in 1852 — a full two decades of seeming financial independence. Through those years, she purchases the usual supplies from the Company store: furnace oil, cloth, sugar, tobacco, rum, biscuits, tea, coffee, and various sundries. However, on occasion, she also pays for the rental of a small boat, passage on a couple of voyages, and transfers amounts to various men in the community. Her sources of income include an impressive array of items: top-grade cured cod, inferior cured cod, whole cod, cod liver oil, haddock, dog fish, seal blubber and pelts, sheep and potatoes. At one point, she is even paid wages for a month's service on one of the Company's ships, the Young Witch. Who was this woman?

As soon as I finished reading, I went to the University of Cape Breton website, looked up Robert Campbell's number in the faculty directory, and called him. When he answered, I told him I'd just found his blog entry and was excited to read about Marie Madeleine Bois, the ancestor I was researching at that very moment.

"She's one of my grandmothers, and you've found some fascinating things about her," I said.

He replied with a good-natured laugh, adding, "It's good to know somebody reads the stuff I put online."

He then told me that my timing was fortunate, that he was just putting the finishing touches on an academic article about the Robin Company in Cheticamp, their truck economy methods, and the research he'd done on the ledgers. He said he'd send it right off to me, and suggested I might like to come to the Beaton Institute on the University campus and have a look at the ledgers for myself.

"A perfect idea," I told him, gave my thanks and appreciation for all he shared with me, then phoned the Beaton Institute and made an appointment to visit the following week. The research librarian asked for the dates of the ledgers I wanted to use, and said they'd be ready when I arrived — then added that if I gave her the names I wanted to research, she might have time to help me get a head start on what I wanted to accomplish while I was on campus.

Sydney, Nova Scotia, where the University of Cape Breton campus is located, was founded and settled by Loyalists fleeing the former British colonies after the American Revolution. It's on the eastern side of Cape Breton, and has the no frills look of an industrial town, which it once was. The local architecture is mostly square-shaped, with some curious exceptions. Down by the port, Sydney claims to have the world's largest fiddle. Including the bow, the instrument is 60 feet tall, and is a much photographed attraction for passengers coming in on the cruise ships that stop in its harbor.

When my husband and I arrived in Sydney on our research adventure (he'd been a scientific researcher all his career and thought he might be of some help), we stayed in a fine hotel, recommended by the librarian and owned by the Membertou First Nation—a part of the larger Mi'kmaq tribe. They're an urban group, located about three kilometers from the center of the city. I enjoyed remembering that Membertou was the name of the Chief who dined with Samuel Champlain and the early French explorers with *L'Ordre de Bon Temps* in the Port Royal *Habitation*.

The University of Cape Breton campus is a red brick cluster of buildings with about 3,000 students—17 percent of them from outside Canada. It's in a beautifully wooded area, and on the day we visited, the leaves were in full autumn reds and golds at their peak.

Once inside the Institute's main room, there were two library carts with six large leather ledgers waiting for us. The heftiest ones were hanging over the edge of the cart. Their leather bindings were an aged fawn color, with scratches and some fraying interrupting the decoration that was tooled around the edges.

They all looked like a ledger Bob Cratchit, Tiny Tim's father in *A Christmas Carol*, would have been writing in—bent over, and perched on his tall stool. Charles Dickens wrote his Christmas novella in 1843, and the Robin Company ledgers I was most interested in were from 1856.

The procedure used by the Robin Company was that at the end of each day, transactions from the daily receipts were compiled and entered into the massive ledgers I was looking at. The recording was done by the young men the Company brought over from the Isle of Jersey. They're written in French, and the script is faded, elaborate and difficult to read. The research librarian apologized to us, saying she wasn't much help, because she had difficulty reading any of it—but she did add slips of paper to the pages of the account holders I had told her were of interest to me.

It was a start, so I picked up the first of the ledgers, which must have weighed 7 or 8 pounds, set it down on a work table, and guided by the paper slips, opened up to a page of the account of *The Widow of Hubert O'Quin.* I expected to begin collecting information, but reading the page was so difficult, I didn't know how to start.

The librarian, my husband, and I all hovered over the pages in dazed bewilderment. Finally, I said maybe I should call Robert Campbell and ask him for advice. He could probably give us a procedure — something to get us started. When I called, he answered right away, asked me if I was at the Institute, then said he'd be right over.

His bright smile was encouraging, and he helped us find the names of the men Marie Madeleine was paying wages to. As far as I could tell, they were not related to her. But in the end, there was no standard procedure to follow. We then thought we could just browse the books, see where the records took us, and maybe, we'd get used to the script, translate some words, and get a feel for the items the people of Cheticamp were buying and selling. Robert stayed with us for awhile and answered all our questions about the Robin Company. He also gave us further information about the nature of the truck society, saying he was exploring whether or not it was essential to the livelihood of the Acadian fishermen, rather than just exploitive of them. In Cheticamp, I only heard the sentiment that the Robin Company was exploitive of the Acadian people, but because of the "Jerseys," as the Robin Company was called, the Acadians were eventually highly motivated to participate in a co-operative movement, providing them ownership in the businesses they frequented.

When Professor Campbell had to leave to teach a class, I turned back to the ledgers and photographed some of the pages on my iPad. At home, I found that when enlarging the images on my home computer and putting them into an editing app to increase the contrast and clarity, I could read some of the accounts with relative ease. After a while, words that were often repeated jumped out at me—*sundries*, *thé* (tea), *tabac* (tobacco), *rhum* (rum), *mélasse* (molasses), *café* (coffee), and *cordage* (rope)—remembering Laurent Molins, the *Religioux Cordelier*/census taker. Time spent with the French to English translation sites on the web helped with words like *ligne* (line), *bouton* (button or knob), *ruban* (ribbon), *chandelle* (candle), *toile* (canvas), *pipes*. Occasionally my high school French surprised me with a translation.

Marie Madeleine had all of the above items and many more on her accounts. She was also charged for renting a shallop, a dory with a sail, often used in the sealing industry. I later found the shallop Marie Madeleine rented by name—*The Young Witch*, officially registered to the Robin company.

It's hard to read about my ancestors harvesting seals. I'm so fond of a herd of them hanging out on the rocks alongside a cluster of cormorants close to our home. We also have a sliver of land on the Tidnish River—a mile's swim up the tidal river from the ocean. One beautiful sunny day, a large seal, stretched itself across the full surface of our little dock, and stayed until the tide turned, then rolled off, and returned to open water. It was in the season when the gaspereau fill the Tidnish River, making it look like the water is dancing. These small fish are in the herring family, and sometimes, in other places, are called alewives. They're used as lobster bait, but seemed to have some appeal to our dock-lounging seal.

The Robin Company ledgers also gave me a glimpse of the lives of my great grandfather, Joseph Burns, married to Agathe Ryan, and Joseph's father, my great-great grandfather, Michael Burns.

On a recent follow-up call to Robert Campbell, he told me that nothing more has been found about Marie Madeleine or her business enterprises. "Many potentially useful documents have either been destroyed or lost— or they're sitting in someone's basement," he said. And so I reluctantly put away my notes on the entrepreneurial and resourceful Marie Madeleine, and moved on.

She and Hubert had nine children, including what is thought to be two sets of twins. Their son Norbert's birth has not been recorded, but he's found with the family on multiple census records. Their children were:

Susanne, born in 1813; twins Monique and Aubeline, 1815; Maurice, 1818; Damien and probably Norbert, 1820; Elizabeth, 1823; Lucille, 1828; and Cecile Nymphe, 1830.

Susanne Aucoin, the oldest of Marie Madeleine Bois and Hubert Aucoin's children, is my third grandmother. She and I were both born on the same day in August.

Susanne Aucoin

Born
1813, Cheticamp, Cape Breton, Nova Scotia

Died
1901, Margaree, Cape Breton

Daughter of
Marie Madeleine Bois
b. 1794, Cheticamp, Cape Breton Island
d. 1884, Cheticamp, Cape Breton Island
Hubert Aucoin,
b.1791
d. about 1832, at sea, Cape Breton Island

Spouse
Thomas Ryan
b.1807, place unknown
d. after 1854
Son of
Elizabeth Desrabis
b. 1770, Montreal, Quebec
d. after February 4,1840,
the date of a daughter's wedding
Joseph Ryan
b. 1773, place unknown
d. 1829, place unknown

By this time in my research and travels, I was getting to know Cheticamp and the small villages around it. I'd driven the coastline so often, I knew the landmarks, and many adventures into the hidden and more remote locations rounded out my sense of the place. Charlie Dan helped me locate where the Robin Company once owned a significant block of land for its operations, and where the cabins had been for the fishermen to sleep in during their workweek. I'd walked my dogs on Cheticamp Island's beach, and spent idle time photographing the harbor view, and the cows that wandered on the road to the lighthouse.

My time with census records and family names moved me to a point where I no longer needed a laminated card full of ancestor data hanging around my neck. But I was lamenting the fact that I had no historical map like the one that guided me to the family home sites up and down the Annapolis River in Port Royal. That is, until I started looking into the family of the man Susanne Aucoin, my third grandmother, married.

Her husband was Thomas Ryan, and well into my online search, I found a reference to a large grant of land given to Joseph Ryan, father of Thomas Ryan. With just a few clicks, I was linked to a Cape Breton land-grant plan showing property ownership in the entire Cheticamp area from the earliest Acadian settlers onward. I spent hours pouring over it, because the many holdings of land belonging to five generations of my Cape Breton ancestors were all there on its brown and aged-looking surface. With the site plan, I could now scan the whole area and see where the earliest families settled, and how they clustered and divided their land to include offspring. I also saw large grants that were shared by multiple people, and could observe which families lived close to each other. I could even speculate on how couples might have met and later married, based on where they lived.

Susanne Aucoin's family owned property in the earliest settlements in and around Cheticamp, but an exception was 230 acres granted to Anselm O'Quin and Raphael Aucoin in Belle Cote, north of Margaree, and adjacent to the property where Susanne's husband Thomas lived as a child. Both the Ryan and O'Quin properties have extensive coastlines, and I wondered if this is where the couple met.

Most of the land grants in the area were for 200 acres, but Thomas Ryan's father, Joseph, had 450 acres south of Cheticamp and north of Margaree. It's by far the largest grant of any of the others in the area. In addition, Basil, the oldest Ryan son, has 205 acres, and sons Jean and Thomas each owned 100 acres—all adjacent to their father's property. Combined, that makes 855 Ryan acres surrounded by mostly Acadian settlers.

In 1818, the missionary, l'abbe Lejamtel recorded the inhabitants of all the households between Cheticamp and Margaree, including the women and children by name. At the bottom of his enumeration, he separated out a location he called *Between Margaree and Cheticamp* and listed the sole inhabitants of this place as Joseph Ryan and his wife, Elizabeth Darabie,(Desrabis) and their eight children: Basile, Joseph, Brigette, Marie, Jean,

Catherine, Thomas, and Louise. Thomas, the next to the last child, would become Susanne Aucoin's husband.

When researching the Acadian people, it's an advantage that the married women are identified by their birth surnames throughout their lives. It's also common that their parents' names are included to help identify them. This information is especially important before marriage. Since it was such a small population, clergy examined the genetic relationships of couples to check *sanguinity*—making sure any cousin relationships were not too close, and giving dispensations whenever possible.

With males, the Acadians often put in parenthesis the male forefathers going back to the first male ancestor who came from France to Nova Scotia. The same thing is not done as often with women, and when it is, the connections go through the male line.

Turning back to my love affair with the Cape Breton land grant plan—the more time I spent with it, the longer my list of questions about interpreting it grew. But, after two phone calls and two emails from the research librarian at the Nova Scotia Bureau of Resources, every question I asked was answered.

My initial problem was figuring out how much land each family owned. On the plan, there was a sentence that read, "One inch equals forty chains." I couldn't figure out how that could help me, looking at the map on a computer screen. And what was a chain? A quick search let me know that a chain is 66 feet, 22 yards, 100.084 links, or 4 rods (20.1168 meters) and that there are 10 chains in a furlong, 80 chains in one statute mile, and that an acre is the area of 10 square chains (or one chain by one furlong). Help!

Just when I had all that memorized (only kidding), the librarian told me that a number plus a couple of letters printed on each plot that I thought was some sort of internal code was actually the number of acres each owner had. She also told me that the document I was using was prepared in the 1920s and thirties, compiled from an assortment of old ledgers and was last updated in 2009.

On the plan, I found the notations and position of the earliest grant of 7,000 acres issued to the original *Fourteen Old Ones* of Cheticamp. I knew the land was given in the names of the 14 who applied to the Crown, and the government left it to the Acadians to divide the acreage among themselves, but I've never found anything written about how they accomplished dividing and giving out the land, or who did all the measuring with chains.

My eyes moved around all of *Sheet 120–Inverness County*–taking in Cheticamp, *Petit Étang, Belle Marche, Plateau, St. Joseph du Moine, Grand Étang, Terre Noir, Belle Cote* and Margaree. The Cabot Trail is clearly marked and so is the land designated to become the Cape Breton Highlands National Park. The individual properties are mostly divided into long, narrow parcels, in the style of the old French *arpents*—giving many people ocean frontage with deep swaths of land going back to the hills. *Arpentage*, from *arpent* is the French word for surveying.

During all the years between Apolline Arseneau's arrival and my grandmother Nelly's leaving Cape Breton, all the women in my Acadian lineage married, had children, and created lives in and near Cheticamp. Not surprisingly, families clustered together, and the younger members, after marriage, were allocated a back portion of the family's acres.

On the land grant plan are the names I heard on my grandmother's porch, others, because they married one of my foremothers, and now, many of the rest, because at this point I've scoured census, birth, and death records, and a goodly collection of miscellaneous Cheticamp documents.

Now that I've learned about the dealings of the infamous Robin Company I'm interested to find the land they controlled on Cheticamp Island. While searching the company, I found a court document involving Appoline's sister, Adelaide, her husband, Basil Chiasson, and the Robins. In it, the company was trying to remove the couple from land they had leased. Robin lost that case, and I later found a document showing the Crown trying to reclaim land from the Robin Company. I needed a lot of help to decipher the first document, which I found online in French. Enlisting some of my French-speaking friends for the translations provided a good time for us all, but I can't say we cracked the case. We all agreed, though, that there's some fascinating history to be learned through the documentation and disputes of property issues.

I have a copy of the grant for Joseph Ryan's 450 acres, which I purchased from the Nova Scotia Bureau of Resources. It's dated the 19th of April, 1814, as a Crown Lease, but no money or conditions are listed. The language of the grant is full of antiquated references, written in the most legible handwriting I've found on any documents thus far. It starts,

A Lot of land beginning on the shore on the Southern side of a cove about 20 chs to the Southward of a run of water at a blazed fir — then continues with more chains, (one direction has 102 of them). There are many compass references, and the description ends with — *reserving also a Road half a chain wide leading from the mouth of (the) Margaree River towards Cheticamp.*

I can't leave the subject of land ownership without thinking about the original people of the area who wandered freely, setting up encampments according to the seasons—the native Mi'kmaq. Starting with the Paleo-Indians, native peoples have been in Cape Breton for about 10,000 years, and today there are five Aboriginal communities living there; the Wagmatcook, Waycobah, Chapel Island, Eskasoni and Membertou. Before Europeans arrived, it's thought that some of these tribes may have camped in the summers on the shores, near Cheticamp, to hunt and fish, then moved inland to winter further from the coast. I wonder if they also camped by the winding Margaree River, renowned for its salmon.

These native people also followed the caribou herds around Nova Scotia. There are sites through the Maritime provinces where artifacts have been naturally exposed by the tides. I was surprised to learn of one of them that's close to my house. It's a burial site on the bank of a tidal river named the Shinimicas, meaning *shining water* in Mi'kmaq. Many years ago, I did a large painting near the location where these Mi'kmaq artifacts were found, without knowing of its native history.

My husband and I have walked the coastline near the Aucoin and Ryan family holdings in *Belle Cote*. The lands running down to the sea are mostly cleared now, and I'm sure that blazed fir tree mentioned in the grant description is no longer standing. But the area is strikingly beautiful still, and further north we've sat on high, wild-rose covered cliffs, watching pilot whales lazily hanging out just off shore.

Closer to the Ryan and Aucoin properties, when one of our walks was underway, our dog, Louie, chose to turn and head in the opposite direction, so I followed him while my husband continued on. Louie and I investigated some coves, then turned back and spotted my husband coming towards us carrying a five-foot long object. When we met up, I could see that he actually had two curved bones—well worn and ivory-colored. Immediately, we referred to them as the *whale bones*, the largest objects we beachcombers have ever found. We've never had their identity verified, and back in Tidnish they lie on top of a long dresser, waiting for us to bring them to someone who will know what they are. Or maybe they're there, as a mystery from a beautiful place, reminding us that not everything has to be named.

Yet I continue to go on looking and naming people and documenting what I find. I'm not satisfied, though, with just having names and dates and locations. Maybe it's because I'm so visual — I want to see the places where they lived, take in the colors and contours of the land, imagine my foremothers walking on it with big bellies waiting for the next child to be born, and their men fishing in the calm or fury of the ocean. That's what brings me the true connections I'm looking for.

Thinking of Susanne Aucoin and Thomas Ryan, I imagine them by the sea, in the place known as *La Cote a Betsy*—where my husband found the bones. When the couple's family was complete, they had nine children — Marie Agathe, Denis, Hubert, Catherine, Esustade, Caroline, Helene-Josephe, Joseph and John. Marie Agathe, their first child, is my great grandmother. She's the first woman ancestor I have without an Acadian surname, and I'm faced with a dilemma. Can I call all the women in my ancestral line Acadian women? *My Acadian grandmothers?*

Sorting it out, I'm reminded of one of my first trips to Cheticamp, and the Acadian woman demonstrating rug hooking. When I told her that my grandmother was from the area, and said that it was not an Acadian name—that it was Burns. She told me that around there, that's considered to be an Acadian name. She was also the one who sang the praises of my cousin, Edmond Burns, as a great genealogist, and sent me to see him. After Edmond died, I asked Charlie Dan if Edmond considered himself to be Acadian.

"Definitely, yes," he answered. "100 percent."

And at a French fort, a guide from a northern New Brunswick Acadian community said she had many neighbors back home named McDougal, and other Irish sounding names who spoke only French, and considered themselves to be Acadian. A Burns relative from Margaree once told me that anyone living between Cheticamp and Margaree Harbour at the time my ancestors lived there, was considered to be French and Acadian. Following up, and looking through the Cheticamp area census, there are many people with Irish names who say their parents were from Ireland, and report that they speak English and French, but list their language spoken at home as French. All of the outside sources present a case for the Acadian cultural impact on my ancestors carrying Irish names. Mothers passing on their heritage and speaking their native language starting at their children's births.

But most important, when my grandmother was married to Frederick Boudrot, and living in the United States, she appears on the 1920 census along with Fred. Both of them say they are from Canada, their mother tongue is French, and that they can speak English. The couple also give French as the language spoken by their parents, and list French as the language of the parents beside the names of each of their own children's names.

I have no doubt that Nelly was culturally French Acadian—*an Acadian Grandmother.* And me, finding my Acadian origins, I realize how strong my own Acadian connection is.

Marie Agathe Ryan

Born
1836, Margaree, Cape Breton Island, Nova Scotia

Died
Margaree, Cape Breton Island, Nova Scotia

Daughter of
Susanne Aucoin
b. 1813, Cape Breton Island, Nova Scotia
d. 1904, Cheticamp, Cape Breton Island, Nova Scotia
Thomas Ryan
b. 1807, Margaree, Cape Breton Island, Nova Scotia
d. about 1854

Spouse
Joseph Burns
b. 1823, Cape Breton Island, Nova Scotia
d. 1907, Cape Breton Island, Nova Scotia
Son of
Elizabeth Booth
b. unknown, Cape Breton Island, Nova Scotia
d. before 1827
Michael Byrne
b. about 1791
d. 1829, Chimney Corner, Cape Breton Island,
Nova Scotia

Opening the bright red cover of the November/December 2006 issue of *The Participaper* (yes, *Participaper*) from Inverness County, Cape Breton, revealed rich material about my great-grandmother, Agathe Ryan's family. Beneath the photos of three familiar genealogists—my cousin, Edmond Burns, Jean Doris LeBlanc, and the now very familiar Charles D. Roach, was an article about the Ryans written by Charlie Dan. The title immediately caught my attention:

Former Family Names That Have Now Disappeared From the Region of Cheticamp–
RYAN
The Enthralling Story of Elisabeth Desrabis

Elisabeth Desrabis married Joseph Ryan. Their son Thomas, married Susanne Aucoin, and their first child was my great-grandmother, Agathe (pronounced *A-get*).

In the *Participaper article*, Charlie Dan wrote:

Around the time of the American Revolution (1776), and for reasons unknown to us, the Desrabis family from Montreal moved to Arichat, on Cape Breton Island. At the time, Elisabeth was still a little girl. She grew up in Arichat where she resided until her twenties. (Later in the article, information is found to show she was actually seventeen at this time.)

Charlie Dan continues:

It was there that she experienced a misadventure that we would not hesitate, by modern standards, to classify as criminal and personally traumatic: She was kidnapped from her parents and tricked into marrying against her will.

In 1802, the l'abbe Champion wrote to the Roman Catholic Bishop of Quebec regarding this matter:

Elisabeth de Reby (sic), originally of Mont Real (sic), was brought as a child to this town called Richat (sic), in Cape Breton, by her father and her mother, who have raised her in the said place until she reached the age of twenty or twenty-one. It is at that age that la Reby (sic) was removed from Rischat (sic) by a Protestant named Daniel Josse, whom she had met at some previous time, and here is how this removal took place: Josse had sent a black woman to tell la Reby (sic) that she should go to the shore to a location that she indicated and to which she led her, telling her that she would find there two persons whom she would be delighted to meet and talk with; when La Reby got there, she discovered Jossse and another man who had come in a little boat to meet her.

Josse approached the Reby girl, took her by the hand and guided her to his boat, as much by force as by persuasion; when they reached the boat, Josse made her get in, more by force than by consent... As soon as she was in the boat, Josse and his comrade started rowing out to sea and reached a village 10 to 12 leagues away, called Merigomiche where he took the girl before a Justice of the Peace who married her according to English law, persuading her that her honor would be lost if she did not go through with the marriage.

The piece goes on to tell how distraught Elisabeth was, how Josse brought her to a missionary priest who married them, and 16 days after this marriage, Josse went to sea to fish oysters in the vicinity of the Magdalen Islands and he and his crew never returned. Six years later,

Elisabeth, assuming that Josse was dead, married Joseph Ryan before a Justice of the Peace.

In 1802, when l'abbe Champion wrote for advice from the Bishop of Quebec regarding the validity of this second marriage in the eyes of the church, he told the Bishop that since Elizabeth's marriage to Joseph Ryan, four children had been born and were always denied the right to receive the sacraments. My great grandmother, Agathe, would have been among the four children who were refused.

The Bishop's response is not known, but can be assumed, since the last of Elisabeth's children was baptized and all nine of the Ryan children were eventually married in a Catholic church.

Charlie Dan's article goes on to include the names of all nine Ryan children. Of those who survived and stayed in the area, he tells who they married, and concludes the article by saying:

The list of the children of Joseph Ryan and Elisabeth Desrabis, presented above, clearly shows how well the Ryans have integrated themselves into the Acadian population of the region of Chéticamp,

St Joseph du Moine and Margaree. Even to the present day, many of the Acadians of this area have Ryan and Desrabis blood running through their veins — in spite of the fact that the names themselves have pretty well vanished.

Agathe's mother, *S*usanne Aucoin, married into a family with an unusual history, and her union with Thomas Ryan probably took place at *Saint Pierre's* church in Cheticamp, Susanne's home parish. Thomas owned 100 acres of land in Belle Cote — perhaps he received it when he married Susanne. He was granted the land in a parcel along with his brothers Basil and John, and a Simon LeBlanc or White in 1841. The official land document begins with:

Victoria, by the Grace of God, (William the Fourth is crossed out and replaced in eloquent script by *Victoria, sic*) *of the United Kingdom of Great Britain and Ireland, Queen* (King crossed out, sic), *Defender of the Faith, and of the United Church of England and Ireland, on Earth the Supreme Head.*

TO ALL TO WHOM THESE PRESENTS SHALL COME, KNOW YE THAT WE, of our

*special grace, certain knowledge and mere motion
have given and granted, by these presence for Us,
our Heirs and Successors, do give and grant unto…..*
The names of the four men are listed, followed
by detailed descriptions of the boundaries of
the land involved. It's signed by "Falkland,"
an Englishman who was the governor of Nova
Scotia from 1840-1846.

There were conditions to the grant. The
grantees were obliged to drain and clear
three acres of swampy and sunken ground for
every 50 acres they received, or drain three
acres of marsh if there were such conditions
on the assigned land. Each was to take place
within three years. There were also conditions
regarding keeping *neat* cattle (an Old English
farming word meaning domesticated cattle) per
50 acres while the land was being cleared and,
when said acreage was in condition, there were
regulations regarding the cultivation of hemp
and flax.

The government clearly wanted the land
to be improved and used, and if, after the
legally stated periods of time for clearing and

cultivating arrived, and all conditions were not met, then the granted land would revert back to the Crown—meaning the government. On the land grant plan showing properties from Cheticamp to Margaree, there are multiple parcels of land around the Ryan property that had been reclaimed by the government. But Agathe's family must have fulfilled all the legal obligations that came with their grant, and I can see where she probably spent her childhood.

I also know that she was eventually confirmed at *Saint Michael's* Church in East Margaree, and married Joseph Burns, who grew up on family property near her own. Agathe and Joseph had 11 children.

When I was searching through the Robin Company ledgers after discovering the *Widow of Hubert Aucoin,* I looked ahead to the year 1856 and found an entry page for Joseph Burns. The ledger entry was less than a page long and filled with purchases under the category of sundries, then coffee, rum, and other mostly unreadable (to me) items. It only had a few entries about fish.

Joseph grew up on the land granted to his father, Michael Byrne, in 1835, He was given the same obligations to improve the land or lose it as the Ryans were. But theirs was different because it required payment—which was peppercorns! Actually, only one peppercorn per year.

Sitting alone by the fire one night, with copies of land-grant documents stacked beside me, I decided I would read every part of each one. The house was quiet, and dark, except for my light. When I was reading the Michael Byrne grant and got to the part about a financial obligation on a described date, or as soon after that date each year as the government would request it, and read that the payment to the Crown was to be one peppercorn. "WHAT?" I said very loud into the dark, reread the sentences several times, then mellowed my voice to say to no one there, "There must be some other peppercorns, rather than the ordinary ones I grind in a mill." I then picked up my iPad and felt silly entering *peppercorns and the law*.

Google came up quickly with more than a dozen entries about peppercorns and contract law. *Wikipedia's* contribution says,

> *To this day, peppercorn is a legal term in English law that represents a small payment or fee simple,* and *Quora,* another site, goes on to explain, *In legal parlance, a peppercorn is a metaphor for a very small payment, a nominal consideration, used to satisfy the requirement for the creation of a legal contract.*

I continued to read, learning that peppercorns were rarely collected according to contract conditions. And I now look at the simple peppercorn and think of its legal history and symbolic international stature. Apparently all the conditions for land ownership required of Michael Byrnes were met—with or without peppercorns—because Joseph Burns and Agathe Ryan lived on the Burns land after they were married. Their 11 children were:

Elizabeth, b. 1861; Dennis, 1862; Thomas, 1863; Suzanne, 1865; Martin, 1867; Luce, 1869; Ellen (Nelly), 1873; Joseph, 1875; John Michael, 1876; and twins, James and Moses, 1878.

Their seventh child, born on the 17th of September, 1873, and baptized on the 7th of October at *Saint Michael's* church in East Margaree, was my grandmother, Nelly.

Hélène, Ellen, Nelly Burns

Born
1873, Friar's Head, Cape Breton Island, Nova Scotia

Died
Newton, Massachusetts 1951

Daughter of
Agathe Ryan,
b. 1837, Margaree, Cape Breton Island, Nova Scotia
d. Margaree, Cape Breton Island, Nova Scotia
Joseph Burns
b. 1823, Cape Breton Island
d. 1907, Cape Breton Island

Spouse
Frederick M. Boudrot
b. 1867, Port Royal, Isle Madame, Nova Scotia
d. 1934. Newton, Massachusetts

Son of
Adele Leblanc
b. Isle Madame, Cape Breton Island
d. unknown
Gaetan Boudrot
b. 1836, Cape Breton Island, Nova Scotia
d. 1913, Cape Breton Island. Nova Scotia

Children of Nelly Burns
and Frederick Boudrot

Gertrude, b. 1904
Raymond, b. 1905
Chester, b. 1907
Melvin, b. 1911
Nelson, b. 1916

There have always been questions surrounding Nelly's name. On census records through the years, and on her death certificate, she's referred to as *Nelly*. On her record of baptism at *Saint Michael's* in East Margaree on Cape Breton Island, she's called *Ellen*, born on September 17, 1873, and baptized by Father Chisholm, a Scottish priest. Her godmother is listed as *Ellen LeBlanc.*

One of the geneaologists at *Les Trois Pignons,* Jean-Doris LeBlanc, told me that it was highly unlikely that an Acadian godmother with a last name of LeBlanc would have Ellen as a first name. Her name was probably *Hélène LeBlanc*. It was also common to name a child after the godparent. The French pronunciation of *Hélène* most likely sounded like *Ellen* to the Scottish priest, and so he wrote it that way—making the infant and the godmother both Ellens. In any case, the baby quickly became Nelly, and remained so all of her years.

On the 144th anniversary of Nelly's birth, in 2017, my husband and I were on one of our many visits to Cape Breton, and I celebrated the day by visiting Nelly's village and attending Mass. She was baptized and attended *Saint*

Michael's in East Margaree. The beautiful brick church was built in 1958, and is the fourth *Saint Michaels* there. The first, a log chapel, was built in 1801, then replaced in 1810. The third church, completed in 1859, was Gothic-style, constructed entirely of wood, and stood for almost 100 years. In 1952, the year after Nelly died, the steeple of the old church was struck by lightning and the structure was leveled in an hour.

When we arrived for Mass on this 144th-year birthday, the parking lot was full, and cars lined all the roads around the church, so my husband dropped me off by the door and went looking for a place to park. I walked inside while the congregation was standing, facing the altar, and reciting something together. There was one empty place in the next to the last row, and I easily slipped in as people were finishing the recitation and taking their seats. The woman beside me gave a warm smile and pulled down the kneeling bench, indicating it was time to pray. After the prayer, we took our seats again, and I had a chance to look around at the congregation, noticing that there was enormous variety in what people wore. Three rows ahead, there was a woman in a black lace dress and shawl, and the man sitting across the aisle wore a red and black checkered shirt. There was all manner of dress, and the quiet outfit I had on that day definitely blended in.

When everyone was settled in their seats, the priest stepped out in front of the altar. He was wearing a long, deep-green garment with the shiny tone of taffeta. His skin was the dark black of someone from the African continent. The priest's grin grew wide as he asked us in a loud voice, "Are you happy?"

We answered in the little weak voices that audiences usually use when they're asked something by a speaker. "Yes," we fluttered.

The priest opened his arms, looked at us intently, and said, in an even louder voice, "Are You Happy?"

We did a bit better this time, raising the pitch of our voices and the level of our enthusiasm. "Yes!" we almost sang, drawing out the "ssssss!"

But we weren't where the priest wanted us to be because he asked us again at full volume, turning his head slowly, taking us all in, "ARE YOU HAPPY?"

"YESSSSSSSS!" we chorused, sending our voices above the beams in the high ceiling, bouncing off the church walls, and emptying our lungs. I now felt relaxed and free of any anxiety I had from being in a strange place, and unsure of how to behave.

I got the priest's message. I was supposed to be HAPPY! I looked around and noticed we were all smiling, and as we quieted, the priest, in a toasty voice started singing, *If you're happy and you know it, clap your hands...* Our clapping must have been satisfactory, because he immediately began giving his homily. Basically, the sermon was a Nigerian boy's coming-of-age story with moral overtones and lessons that were applicable on any continent, in any country, in any religion. Because he brought us all back to childhood with his happy questions and song, we heard his message in the pure context of childhood, and, with him, moved it into our adult lives.

The rest of the Mass continued, and when it was time to take communion, I stepped out of my pew and to the very back of the church. People began lining up behind me, so I left the head of an unintended line and went into the vestry until everyone came back from the altar and was seated. The priest, who was relatively new to the congregation, had another question for us.

He asked us if we thought the Lord worked in mysterious ways. Because we knew enthusiasm was expected of us, we answered YES with gusto. "When I was a baby in Nigeria, the priest who baptized me gave me the middle name of MacDonald — Ibeh MacDonald Ujunwa—and now, here I am in Cape Breton, surrounded by MacDonalds," he chuckled.

I shook hands with Father Ibeh MacDonald Ujunwa as I left the church, then walked around the back and into a door leading to a small room buzzing with activity. There was a gathering around a woman who seemed to be answering an assortment of questions, so I stood nearby and waited to ask her about access to church records—to look up family information. When she asked me the family name, and I told her it was Burns, she said, "You must be related to Wilfred Burns. He was here, today. He had on a blue and white shirt. Did you see him?"

"No," I smiled, and she went on.

"You should go and visit with him. He just got a new cell phone, and I don't have the number to give you, but you could go to his house. He has a red truck and lives in Margaree Harbour. Do you know where Margaree Harbour is?"

"Yes, I know how to get there—I turn off the Cabot Trail at the place where they make the hackmatack cutting boards—right?"

She told me to turn left at that intersection and go into the village and just drive around until I saw a red truck in a driveway. She couldn't tell me exactly how to get to Wilfred's house, but was sure I'd find it.

I thanked her, and outside, I spotted my husband in the now-empty parking lot. I filled him in about Wilfred Burns as we drove in the direction of the Cabot Trail. When we got to the turn for Margaree Harbour, we had to stop and wait to make our left turn, because coming in the opposite direction, and signaling a right turn, was a *red truck*! In unison, we pointed and shouted, then made the turn to follow the truck down the road, into the village, past the United Church, the general store, the boat-filled harbor, and onto several streets, until it turned into a wide driveway.

We stopped and waited on the road until the truck door opened and a man wearing a blue and white shirt got out. I stepped out of the car and called to him, "Are you Wilfred Burns?"

He shifted the plastic bag of parsnips he was carrying, told me that he was Wilfred, and waited while I walked towards him and said, "I think we're cousins."

"Come on in the house," he said, and turning in the direction of my husband waiting in the car, added, "Bring him, too."

Single file, we followed Wilfred through the back door and down his hallway into the bright, open house. Without turning around, he called back to us,

"Don't bother to take your shoes off. I live alone."

The house was neat and minimally furnished, and after putting the parsnips away, Wilfred pulled out some kitchen chairs and offered us seats around his table. I asked a few questions, and Wilfred said he'd better call his brother, Freddie, and take us to his house because he was the smart one in the family, who knew all about genealogy. Before we left Wilfred's, he told us all the Burns family had prominent chins, and that one of them was even nicknamed *Chinny*. I put my hand up to my average-sized chin and wondered about that as we walked down the hall, out the door, and off to Freddie's house.

A few miles down the road, and at the widened entrance to Freddie's driveway, a few people were collecting spring water in large containers from the spigot he had installed for friends and neighbors to use. It was long and steep getting up the driveway, and I wondered what it must be like in the depth of winter.

Freddie and his wife Rose greeted us warmly, and once again, offered us chairs around the kitchen table. The room was spacious, with broad windows and views at each end, a computer and printer in a far corner, a few comfortable chairs, and a larger, more formal table and chairs below the window that looked down the hill and over the Margaree River. We were offered a coffee by Rose, who was Acadian from the northern part of New Brunswick. I liked being there, in the homey kitchen with these friendly people.

Wilfred was right about Freddie. He did know a lot about the Burns family, and quickly cleared up the issue about my lack of a prominent chin as soon as I told him I was definitely related to Edmund Burns.

"You're from the first wife, then," he said. "Elizabeth Booth and Michael Burns had three children before she died. Wilfred and I, and five more, are from the second wife."

He then gathered materials he had about the Burns family, made copies, and gave them to me. One of the items was a map of the area with a designation of where the Burns land was. When I asked him how to get to it, he said it was hard to find, gave us directions, and said if we got lost to stop at the Aucoin's house and they'd know how to help us.

We'd been driving back and forth in the area, definitely lost, when we spotted an attractive white house set back off the Cabot Trail with an *Aucoin* sign on the front lawn. John Aucoin's wife responded to my knock, and when I told her what I was looking for, she opened the door wide and said, "Well, come on in—you'll need to talk with my husband. He's the one from around here."

After our greetings, I took the seat they offered at the dining room table. The house was as warm and inviting as Fred and Rose's, and John confirmed that there was a Michael Burns who once owned all the land up above him, but that another young fellow had it now, and was clearing timber there. John said his uncle used to own the house we were in and that he played all over the land above when he was a boy.

"There used to be an old foundation up there, but it's all overgrown now. There's no way we could even get to it," he explained.

It was late afternoon when I arrived at their house and after John looked out the window to see our car, he said, "That low-slung Prius would never make it up the road. Come back tomorrow afternoon, and I'll drive you up in my SUV."

Leaving the Aucoin house that Sunday, with the promise of a trip up to Nelly's homestead the following day felt like a birthday gift given to me.

We returned to the Aucoin house the next day, and traveled the dirt road heading up the low mountain to a broad view of the sea. There were no visible traces of the Burns, or any family, ever having lived there. But I was carrying the government land-grant map, and the old, hand-drawn one given to me by Freddie Burns—both indicating that we were on Burns land. John Aucoin, as he drove up the steep hill, told me he had seen the original deed, shown to him by the new owner. "Burns was definitely on the deed," he said. To add to it all, Edmund Burns once told me that my ancestors lived beside his family's property, and I could see Edmund's blue house on our way up the road.

Arriving on Nelly's land gave me a powerful feeling that my family search was complete. On the highest point of the rutted road, wooded in every direction, and lined in sections with apple trees heavy with their ripe fruit, everything seemed right—especially the apples. My father was a lover of apples. If you gave him an apple pie, he was wildly happy. In the autumns of my childhood, our Sunday rides often consisted of trips to local, and sometimes distant orchards, to buy his favorites. He always seemed to know when they would be ready for eating.

On this day in Cape Breton, on the way back down the Burns mountain, I felt compelled to stop and pick an apple to taste. The trees were definitely not 150-year-old Burns apples—but maybe the seeds from Nelly's time there made their way into the ground, and grew to seed more trees, continuing the cycle, and somewhere in an apple I might pick, there would be something of the essence of the original in it. As there is Burns in me.

From experience, I knew uncultivated apples growing wild, were not tasty. In fact, an acquaintance who grows apples commercially and sells his cider, calls these uncultivated apples *spitters*.

"You know," he once said, "Standing in the field, picking an apple from the lone tree, you take a bite and are so appalled by its pithy taste, you have no desire to eat the thing, and so you spit it out."

"I know," I said. "I've tasted the ones you're talking about."

Still, my apple-growing acquaintance asked me to try all the ones I told him are in my Nova Scotia field.

"If you ever find one that tastes good, mark the tree and I'll come and use it to graft onto some of mine, and we may produce something wonderful," he added.

Halfway down the Cape Breton/Burns mountain, and before the notched tree that shows itself to be a kilometer from the ocean's high water mark, we stopped and I picked an especially pretty apple off a robust tree and alas, it was a *spitter*. I'd also given John Aucoin and my husband apples from the same tree and, after biting into them, their expressions and actions were the same as mine.

When I moved to the next tree, bit into the apple I picked from it, and said it tasted very good, they were skeptical—thinking I was luring them into trying another bad one. But I kept eating mine, and they said they'd try another one—and after a bite, agreed that they tasted good. Not great, but good.

Every time I've left Cape Breton, as I cross the Strait of Canso into mainland Nova Scotia, I wonder how Nelly felt leaving her beautiful Island. I'm also cloaked in sadness as I cross the deep water, even though I've always known that it's close enough for me to come back.

Nelly never returned to Cape Breton.

Although she lived a full and seemingly happy life outside of the Island, I wonder what it was like for her to leave—for she surely knew that it was too costly and far away from her Massachusetts destination to return. In my mind, on this day, I created the image of her leaving the mountain and the sea, stopping to take it all in, then picking an apple and putting it into her bag to enjoy on the journey.

I reached up and picked another apple from the same tree and held it. When asked if I was going to try it, I said, "No. I'm going to save it till I get across the causeway, and on the mainland. Once I make the crossing off the Island, I'm back to living a busy life." Swooping my arm to include the view of the sea and the land, I said, "I want the apple to remind me to keep all of this with me every day."

At home, I took the saved apple seeds and tossed them into the field behind the house. Not being a great cultivator, I wished them well and wondered if, on their own, they'd grow like the other wild things that appear around the property each spring.

With a cup of tea in hand, I wandered onto the porch, and the dog followed close behind. The sun was shining on one side, so I pulled my chair in that direction to get its full warmth. Louie followed, and curled up on the rug beside me, sharing the spot of sun. I felt content and full from the Cape Breton trip and finding Nelly's land.

There on the porch, I could feel her presence—and the presence of them all. What a journey I'd been on, finding the nine grandmothers—each one so alive and brave. Living through difficult times, and surviving. Gathered here together, I could feel their energy. They laughed and rattled on like Nelly with her Cape Breton friends on her porch back in my childhood. Each of the nine grandmothers had at least one daughter, who had at least one daughter. And sons. One day soon, I'll count all these children and be amazed.

The sun was starting to turn a rippled red. *Red sky at night, sailor's delight,* I thought. *It'll be another good day of calm seas tomorrow.* I stirred in my chair, thinking about what we'd have for dinner, and could feel the women gathering up their things and preparing to leave.

I picked up my empty cup and slid the chair back to its place—the space where they had all been sitting. The dog stood up to see what I was doing, then tensed his ears and turned when he heard the birches rustling with a wind that blew in. He cocked his head, looking in the direction of the water's edge. I leaned against the door frame, dangling the empty cup, and watched as he slowly shifted his gaze, then stared for the longest time towards the sea—the place that was so familiar, and such a part of them all.

ORIGINAL MOTHERS
OF ALL ACADIANS ALIVE TODAY

1 AIMEE, Jeanne (m1 v 1685 Julien Aubois dit Saint-Julien; m2 1719 Julien Guyon dit Saint-Julien).

2. ARNAULT, Marie (m1 v 1688 Jacques Carne; m2 1729 Martin Lejeune dit Briard).

3. AUBOIS, Marie (Christine) (m v 1686 Jean Roy dit Laliberte).

4. AUCOIN, Jeanne (m v 1647 Francois Girouard)

5. AUCOIN, Michelle (m v 1641 Michel Boudrot)

6. BAJOLET, Barbe (m1 v 1629 Isaac Pesseley; m2 1647 Martin Lefebvre de Montespy; m3 1654 Savinien de Courpon)

7. BARTINEAU dit PELTIER, Louise (m v 1684 Louis Saulnier).

8. BASILE, Perrine (m v 1685 Andrd Celestin dit Bellemere).

9. BAYON, Rose (m v 1649 Pierre Comeau)

10. BERNON, Anne (m v 1693 Pierre Lavergne).

11. BERTEAU (BERTRAND), Cecile (m v 1703 Jean Denis).

12. BILLOT, Genevieve (m 1670 Jean Denis)

13. BISSOT, Marie (m1 1682 Claude Porlier; m2 1691 Jacques Gourdeau)

14. BOILEAU, Marguerite (m v 1663 Jean Serreau de Saint-Aubin).

15. BOURG, Perrine (m1 v 1640 Simon Pelletret; m2 v 1645 Rene Landry l'aine)

16. BOURGET, Francoise (m 1714 Jean Doucet)

17. BREAU, Renee (m v 1644 Vincent Brun)

18. BRUNET, Marie (m 1710 Nicolas Pugnant dit Destouches).

19. BUGARET, Catherine (m1 v 1658 Claude Petitpas; m2 v 1692 Charles Chevalier dit LaTourasse)

20. CANOL, Marie-Anne (m v 1671 Jean Doiron)

21. CAPLAN, Catherine (m v 1730 Pierre Huard).

22. CAPLAN, Madeleine (m v 1740 Olivier Michel)

23. CAPLAN, Marguerite (m v 1719 Francois Laroque)

24. CAPLAN, Marie-Louise (m1 v 1729 Francois Hyard dit Saint-Louis; m2 v 1740 Claude-Louis Lalande dit Saint-Louis)

25. CHAUSSEGROS, Marie (m v 1672 Martin Benoit).

26. CHEBRAT, Jeanne (m1 v 1647 Jean Poirier; m2 v 1654 Antoine Gougeon).

27. COLLESON, Nicole (m v 1652 Jean Gaudet)

28. CORBINEAU, Francoise (m 1627 Guillaume Trahan)

29. (D'AMOURS) de CHAUFFOURS, Louise (m v 1703 Jean Auger).

30. DOUCET, ------ (m v 1650 Pierre Lejeune dit Briard)

31. DOUCET, Marguerite (m v 1647 Abraham Dugas)

32. DUGARD, Marie-Antoinette (m 1692 Pierre de Saint-Vincent).

33. FOREST, Genevieve (m1 v 1689 Francois Savary; m2 v 1692 Louis Mazerolle).

34. GAUDET, Francoise (m1 v 1644 ------ Mercier; m2 v 1650 Daniel LeBlanc)

35. GAUDET, Marie (m1 v 1650 Etienne Hebert; m2 v 1676 Dominique Gareau)

36. GAUTHIER, Martine (m v 1645 Denis Gaudet).

37. GAUTROT, Anne (m v 1688 Joseph Pretieux).

38. GUYON, Andree (m1 v 1644 ------ Bernard; m2 v 1651 Antoine Belliveau)

39. GUYON, Louise (m1 1684 Charles Thibault; m2 1686 Mathieu D'Amours de Freneuse)

40. HELIE, Madeleine (m v 1649 Philippe Mius d'Entremont)

41. HENRY, Jeanne (m v 1680 Jean Gaudet).

42. HOUSSEAU, Marguerite (m 1670 Jean Meunier).

43. JAROUSELLE, Susanne (m1 1655 Simon Lereau; m2 1671 Robert Cottard).

44. JEANNE, Andree-Angelique (m 1690 Gabriel Godin dit Bellefontaine).

45. JEAN dit MADELON, Isabelle-Madeleine (m v 1709 Martin Giboire Duverge dit LaMotte).

46. JOSEPH, Cecile (m 1 v1694 Etienne Rivet; m 2 v 1708 Martin Corporon)

47. JOSEPH, Edmee (m v 1696 Charles Chauvet dit LaGerne

48. JUDIC, Madeleine (m v 1660 Jean Huret dit Rochefort)

49. KAGIGCONIAC, Jeanne (m v 1684 Martin Lejeune).

50. LAMBERT, Radegonde (m v 1642 Jean Blanchard

51. LANDRY, Antoinette (m v 1642 Antoine Bourg).

52. LAVACHE, Anne (m v 1712 Louis Labauve).

53. LEFRANC, Genevieve (m v 1648 Antoine Hebert)

54. LEJEUNE, Catherine (m v 1651 Francois Savoie)

55. LEJEUNE, Edmee (m v 1644 Francois Gautrot)

56. LEJEUNE, Jeanne (m v 1673 Francois Joseph)

57. LEJEUNE, Marie-Josephe (m v 1689 Pierre Cellier dit Normand)

58. MARTIN, Marie-Madeleine (c 1683 Guyon Chiasson and 2 c 1693 Michel Deveau dit Dauphine).

59. MICHEL, Jacquette (m1 1660 Jean Gardin and 2 23 October 1668 Andre Mignier dit Lagasse)

60. MOTIN de REUX, Jeanne (m1 v 1638 Charles de Menou d'Aulnay de Charnisay; m2 1653 Charles de Saint-Etienne de La Tour)

61. NICOLAS, Elisabeth (m v 1646 Amand Lalloue)

62. OUESTNOROUEST dit PETITOUS, Anne (m v 1660 Pierre Martin)

63. PATARABEGO, Anne (m v 1680 Richard Denys de Fronsac)

64. PERAUD, Marie (m v 1635 Robert Cormier)

65. PIDDIWAMISKWA, Marie (m v 1685 Jean-Vincent d'Abbadie de Saint-Castin)

66. RAU, Perrine (m v 1636 Jean Theriot)

67. ROUSSELIERE, Jeanne (m1 1654 Pierre Godin dit Chatillon; m2 1686/1693 Pierre Martin)

68. SAINT-ETIENNE de LA TOUR, Jeanne de (m v 1655 Martin d'Aprendestiguy de Martignon)

69. SOUBIROU, Isabeau dite Judith (m v 1685 Pierre Maisonnat dit Baptiste)

70. TOUPIN, Francoise (m avant 1702 Pierre-Paul de Labat)

71. VIGNEAU, Catherine (m 1630 Pierre Martin)

72. -------, ------ (m v 1678 Philippe Mius d'Azy)

73. -------, Anne-Marie (m1 v 1653 ------- Pinet; m2 v 1655 Rene Rimbault)

74. -------, Catherine (m1 v 1680 Jean Labarre; m2 v 1691 Etienne Rivet

75. -------, Marie (m v 1701 Nicolas Denys de Fronsac)

76. -------, Marie (m v 1635 Francois Gautrot)

77. -------, Marie (m v 1687 Philippe Mius d'Azy)

78. -------, Marie-Therese (m v 1686 Claude Petitpas)

79. -------, Mathilde (m v 1670 Jean-Vincent d'Abbadie de Saint-Castin)

80. -------, Priscilla (m1 v 1631 Pierre Melanson dit LaVerdure; m2 1680 William Wright)

List prepared by Steven White, at *Centre d'études acadiennes*

Université de Moncton.